Walking in My Own Divinity

WALKING IN MY OWN DIVINITY

ONE WOMAN'S JOURNEY INTO THE LIGHT

PEMA DEANE

ISBN: 978-0-578-96982-4 (paperback)

Editor: Anandi Ramana

Front Cover Photo: Ilana Block

Snow Geese Photo: Lucille Shiro

Light in Trees Photo: Jennifer Stevens

Interior Photos: Many thanks to all who contributed photographs

Book Jacket Design: Orna Villazan

Book Design and Layout: Aaron Rose, Mount Shasta, California

Published by Walk in Light

For more information, please visit thevibrantheart.typepad.com or email infomagsdeane@gmail.com

Dedication

To all the dear beings that have crossed my path in this life, in small and big ways. You have all blessed me, enriched my life and served me wholeheartedly in guiding me home. I am so grateful to all of you, and I love you.

And to you, dear reader, I am honored if my life experience or words help you in any way on your precious journey home to the Beloved of your Heart.

Contents

2009

2010

2011

2012

2013–2015

2016

2017

2018

2019

2020

2021

APPENDICES

Welcome

The Vibrant Heart is an invitation to let Love have you, to give yourself and your life into the keeping of your own heart, the heart of all Being. So many lives we have lived out in painful separation and now, at last, we are able and willing to respond to the call of the heart, calling us home.

It calls us home persistently, lovingly... and with the greatest of precision and wisdom, it orchestrates the surrender of the personal will so we come to rest with deepest gratitude as the quiet, ease and love that we are.

This journey home, in my experience, is deeply challenging. It is not within the capacity of mind to give itself up easily, and the journey is often experienced as an absolute wearing down process. There is much melting and softening of the ego shell that happens as the heart begins to welcome in all the contracted, defended, unloved parts of ourselves. We gradually, over time, make peace, make tender peace with all of ourselves.

These writings may offer sustenance, nourishment and truth in this process of unwinding and awakening. They are born from my own experiences and come to me in either moments of struggle, expansion or plain truth-seeing. May they speak to you too as we travel together this ever-so-rich, unparalleled terrain of the heart.

Introduction

Writing as a means to deepen my spiritual growth came to me quite unexpectedly in the fall of 2009. I never envisioned myself as a writer nor had any real experience in writing and so it was quite the lovely surprise. Even lovelier was the release and feeling of connectedness to Spirit as I wrote. Often, I would just cry on feeling the beauty of something larger than my normal self-concept move through me and give expression to words and prose that were frequently a carrier of this loveliness.

More often than not, the writing pieces came when I was contracted or triggered. I would be pointed towards a reframing of what was being experienced—a reframing in truth—which brought relief, clarity and a renewed inspiration.

All in all, the writings came to chronicle my journey through many years of dark night spells, beautiful heart openings and on into a resoundingly more solid identification with the truth of my being, the Light and Love that I am. There were periods, years even, where the writing fell away. There was an awareness that the ego was garnering some gratification, specialness, ownership from what was coming through and a subsequent wanting to let that go. Other times, serious illness interrupted, and no writing could happen.

You will notice that the writings are stand-alone pieces. Any page can be opened at any time, and it is complete in itself. The first four years or so were mostly devoted to meeting all that had been repressed in the psyche and the body. Over and over again, I was being reminded to sit with the challenging emotions and sensations. I had several auto-immune disorders during this period, and much of what I wrote about as unresolvable in the life weaved around being unable to find a solution to the physical unwellness.

It may seem at times that there is some contradiction in the pointings. But I came to see that whatever came through in the moment was perfect for me right then. It could point in another direction in another moment, and that too was just perfect for where I was at.

It is my heartfelt prayer that you will find support and inspiration in these pages. That you come to know that everything opens eventually. That a love we've never tasted in these human forms, have so forgotten, eventually comes to the foreground of our hearts, melting all the hard edges and grievances and shut-downs. That the Great Light that you are makes itself known more steadily, more profusely in your everyday life.

You bow down, and you bow down because you never thought such beauty could be yours. All the years of processing and burning and washing out of the small, mythical "me." You are profoundly grateful for all of it, even as it seems to sit in another life.

This Beauty is our fate. Our inheritance. Our incredible God-given inheritance.

Let us make haste here. Giving this chaotic mind of fragmentation back to Heaven with every opportunity and grace-guided moment we have. Heaven is what we are. A state of mind where perfection reigns, and only happiness and goodness see the light of day. The light of God. Our immortal reality.

A Portrait of Pema

Throughout my life I was always trying to feel better about myself. Be better, be more important, be significant, special in some way. This would bring happiness and peace, surely. What a well-worn dogma for all ego selves.

On my first trip to India when I was already in my fifties, there was a clear seeing into the make-up of this mind and this particular dynamic. It was 2007 and the three-week long Deeksha program at the Oneness University with Sri Bhagavan and Amma was calling many Westerners. One of the days there, I was graced with a "Deeksha" (a concentrated blessing of light) that offered a very deep experience and seeing.

I became aware of a very disturbed feeling in my system, and the word that kept coming was "insignificance." I could feel how the baseline of this self-concept, this small "me," was a strong belief in insignificance. It was dreadfully uncomfortable, and to make matters worse, it felt like there was no way out of it. The belief seemed to be encased in a slab of cement, just not penetrable. The cement walls were held in place by the belief that "I am a sinner."

I recoiled at this. I never liked the word "sin," mostly on account of my strong Catholic upbringing in Ireland. I left the Church, so to speak, at fourteen as so much of life seemed to dance around the concept of sin.

Images appeared of myself as a small child doing the Stations of the Cross—pictures of Jesus dying on the cross for my sins—so the theology went. I could see this was literally taken into this small child's mind as a belief that "I am a sinner," and so I must suffer.

It is hard to take in that these strange beliefs get embedded in children's minds, but indeed they do. Even more surprising is to realize that this heaviness was already in place in the unconscious mind. The belief in sin did not start with the Catholic Church's doctrine but stemmed from the believed separation from God. I, as a collective ego mind, had left my Father, broken Heaven up and had committed the most grievous wrong. This was the original sin. But only in imagination.

Being graced with this deep experience, I thought these beliefs in sin and insignificance were being dissolved just in the seeing of them. Not so. It still took many, many years of processing and unraveling to lighten and undo these false beliefs. This made way, thankfully, for truth, for the realization that these mental beliefs have no substance or credence in the heart of God. There is no such thing as unworthiness, no such thing as sin. The heavy mantle of mind is lifted, and what remains to shine? Only our absolute beauty and innocence.

In hindsight and sitting where I sit today, it's so clear I came into this life to undo these false, egoic beliefs and to know myself as Light and Love. It all had to play out just as it did, and I, of course, knew nothing about what was driving the storyline, what was spawning all the striving and searching to feel better.

I grew up in a small village in rural Ireland in the fifties and sixties. Between being the youngest of seven, my father being a strong authority figure and the influence of the Catholic Church, the persona of Margaret (my birth name) was molded into one who felt safe staying small, not making any waves and generally showing up as a good, kind, unselfish person. The dampening down of spirit and general repression led to a character who felt insecure and unworthy.

In my early twenties I left Ireland and moved to Montreal, got married, had two beautiful daughters and a career teaching English as a Second Language. On the surface of life, this looked good, but a growing internal anxiety was making itself known. My need for God and a spiritual life was rising. I remember going around visiting different churches at this time, but nothing spoke to me. It was just a repeat of the priests of my childhood speaking from a pulpit that just didn't touch my heart.

It was when I started having panic attacks going into the classroom as a teacher that my journey got all my attention. I prayed so sincerely one night, an on-your-knees-to-God prayer. God, if you exist, please help me. A short time later, I found myself in the welcoming arms of a perfect therapist, an older woman in her seventies, ninety per cent blind and so attuned and sensitive to what I needed. A lot of repressed emotion came up to be released. I started to feel lighter and a tad freer.

At this stage I was exploring New Age spirituality in a big way, and for many years, I was giving talks and workshops on these topics. This helped my confidence and worth base a lot, and yet the striving continued. I still believed that success in the outer world would bring me happiness.

Out driving one day I noticed I was comparing myself to John Bradshaw, a well-known seminar leader in personal development. My mind had such a tendency to compare and compete and come up short. It was exhausting. I remember being so distraught that I pulled over to the side of the road and some kind of surrender happened. Slumped over the steering wheel, a deep prayer for peace burst forth. I just wanted peace.

This was a pivotal moment as I drove right away to the nearest metaphysical bookstore and bought a copy of *A Course in Miracles.* I had heard good things about this Course and how its goal was peace of mind. I was finally on a more direct path to God.

It wasn't long after that, that a new kind of shock rippled through my psyche. My husband was diagnosed with an aggressive brain cancer and the next four years until he passed were a huge wearing down and waking up time. The intensity of it all, the arduous caretaking, the grief, the vulnerability were all a catalyst for the breaking down of protective, egoic layers and the softening and mellowing out of my being.

Just a short year after the passing of my husband, Jesús—yes, ironically, my husband's name was Jesus, a not uncommon name in Spain where he came from—I was catapulted into my next big learning: the romantic, special, love relationship. Naively, I believed I had worked through so much in those challenging years with my first husband, that relationship after that would be a lot more peaceful to navigate.

How wrong I was. How little the mind knows. The truth is that our deeper beliefs are hidden from us until we become quite mature and can tell from the nature of our thoughts in the conscious mind what beliefs are underneath that are spawning these thoughts. I had a lot of limiting beliefs from my culture and ancestry that a woman needed a man to survive in the world—financially and as some kind of protector. This got to come to the surface in the next few years and be undone.

Aside from my studies with *A Course in Miracles* at this time, I had also started to do silent retreats with non-dual teachers in the tradition of Ramana Maharshi, such as Gangaji, which expanded later into time with Adyashanti and Byron Katie. All profoundly helpful in the unraveling of the egoic mind. On one of these retreats with Gangaji, I met someone and fell in love like a besotted teenager.

It was a tumultuous time. This man had come out of a long marriage and was unsure of what he wanted. And I was crazily grasping at love outside myself and feeling the full ache of what that brings up in the human system. And also experiencing the other extreme: the special love relationship in the moments when it's working, it really works. I can remember how heady it felt at times to be in this special kind of cocoon with my partner. Just he and I. I felt so special and loved. It's no wonder *A Course in Miracles* calls this the strongest defense against the Truth because it is the place that most mimics and replays our relationship with God. Safety and love.

But, of course, it cannot last as a substitute for God's love because the experience is dependent on something outside us.

It took many years for all this fascination and dependency on another to undo itself. This included marriage to this person, a move to Portland, Oregon from Montreal, Quebec and later, a painful divorce. But the rooting out of this very strong egoic defense seemed to be complete. There was no longer any interest or thoughts in that direction. The master of exquisite orchestration, the Holy Spirit, the One who knows exactly what we need, had been in charge of it all.

Devaji, a non-dual teacher had started giving satsang (meetings in Truth) when I first arrived in Portland. He was to become a very important figure in my life, playing out different aspects for me. A wonderful, deeply realized guide into the Truth for me and also the holder of some strong egoic projections on my part. I got to know Devaji socially first; he was a friend of my husband's. I felt intimidated by and fearful of him from the get-go, although he only came to me with great love and goodwill. For many years I would pay an occasional visit to his satsang to see if it was a fit for me. I would always imagine that I could see some ego in him and go away feeling kind of satisfied. How little I understood then that I was only seeing my own mind being projected back to me.

In time, I finally joined Devaji's community and came into another period of deep healing, slowly working through projections onto members of the community. The competing, comparing program of my mind had to be worked on and seen through over and over again. The egoic character wanted to be special: to be the most evolved, the most loving, the most loved. Every which way I would turn in the mind, I would come up short. Feeling less than or, of course at other moments, feeling superior. It was amazing how much this played and how long it took to have this form of separation washed out of my system: the ongoing watching of the falsity of these beliefs and the handing of them over to my Holy Self for correction.

Devaji replayed the dynamic I had with my father and authority figures in general. I had placed them on a pedestal as having more power than me, so all of that had to come down so I could be in the essential Truth of equality of being.

At the same time as the mind was being burned away, there was more joy and love and lightness of being moving in. True connection with others was happening. I was finding my way, and trust in the overall journey was growing.

One of those years I took a trip to the jungles of Peru to explore healing with the plant medicine, ayahuasca. This was such a revelatory time for me, as the deeper truths of reality and existence were shown to me. I saw how, in Truth, there was no individual character at all; how the world was a dream, a vast illusion, how nothing had ever happened, and that we had never left our Source. There was also a profound experience of Love, an unforgettable experience that left no doubt as to how adored I was, how adored all of us are. Every single thing about us is adored. And the habits and behaviors that the character felt ashamed of were equally loved if not even with a greater effect, as it was so profoundly touching to feel the Love pouring into these areas.

And then sickness came to play, to make sure I would go all the way or as far as possible in this life. In 2015 I was diagnosed with breast cancer and a year later it had metastasized to the bone. Over the next six years I was to experience many different states of sickness, from being on hospice twice and needing a lot of caretaking to periods where I could manage more daily tasks by myself. It has been an intense and challenging time and also immensely freeing.

A lot of vulnerability and fragility came to pass and, over time, opened my heart in the most beautiful way. Many tears at moments, old energies releasing, not knowing really what was being cleansed but aware that there was a new softness growing in my heart. The beautiful Love that we are was being experienced more regularly. There was also a great push to shift identification from the body to the Self, to the Light of God. This is an ongoing process.

Numerous lessons were learned along the way. Initially there were choices, decisions to be made around what kind of treatment was right for me, following my heart around this and learning to stand up to different doctors and surgeons. Being true to my own guidance now was a far cry from the automatic way of responding to the authority figures of my childhood.

Hopelessness and despair presented themselves regularly, and I came to see that these states were already inside me. The circumstances of a dysfunctional body were the outpicturing of these states in the dream world. It always seems as though the circumstances are the cause of the emotional states, but actually they are the effect. The dark states of mind, the energetics, are already in the unconscious mind arising from the pain of the believed separation from our Source, and they are the cause of the karmic outpicturing: in my case, sickness. It was very challenging at times being with this sense of hopelessness, but it was also freeing to know that a serious karmic cleansing was happening.

I leaned heavily on the nondual teaching and that of *A Course in Miracles* that the script is already written, and this brought peace and relief at many moments. That karmically, the life scenario was already laid out, and I was walking through it. This is not to say that we do nothing or don't try to make changes. It just means that any changes that occur are already part of the script. Anything I was meant to do, I would be doing it.

Off and on, there were outbursts of grief as I contemplated physical death and the leaving of loved ones. Grief, as is true for every emotion and state, does not go on forever, and it gradually eased until I could imagine leaving with a kind of knowing that I couldn't leave anybody as we were all one in spirit. A sweet sensing of the Truth of this.

I would also feel attracted to death as a way out of this sickness that seemed incurable. Such a normal human response, but I knew this wasn't the answer either. I knew that the death of the body wouldn't take me out of dreaming and illusion. Only the Truth could do that. I kept and keep giving this attraction to death back to the Holy Spirit and relax as best I can into the spacious awareness, into the unknown. Not knowing what is to happen or what is best for my soul feels so good.

At this time of writing, I am under hospice care. The functionality of the body is limited, but my life feels rich. Each day, each week, there is a deepening into the Love that we all so truly are. Mind still arises with its favorite, separating thoughts, but they are all milder and softer. And with every opportunity I give this mind back to Heaven, where it rightfully belongs, at the foot of Source. At the altar of Source. The intention is for every thought that brought about time and illusion and the dream of a Pema character to be safely tucked away and disappear into the Light of God.

Editor's Note

The editor has attempted to remain true to Pema's creative expressions and unique ways of speaking. You will find some novel "new" words within this book. Also, please understand that certain apparent inconsistencies in the use of initial capitals is intended to remain true to Pema's intention in each instance.

2009

Tenderness, Inch by Glorious Inch

"God's heart is more gentle than the Virgin's first kiss upon the Christ."

~ St. Catherine of Siena

October 8

Some years back when I was living in Portland, Oregon, I was trying to find my way around the Pearl District. I had lived in this city for eight years, and this part was still a messy maze to me.

Nothing new about this. All my life I have felt disoriented in a world of one-way streets, stop signs at this corner and not the next, cars behind me wanting me to go faster. On this occasion, quite reliably, I noticed feelings of overwhelm and fragility arrive. Thoughts of *this world is too much for me. I'll never get better at this stuff…* all start filling up the screen of my consciousness. I want to be at home, safe in my own house and I especially want to be away from what's going on in my nervous system.

As I start sinking into this whirlpool of conditioned mind, images of my mother arise… her lost, scared, befuddled face on leaving a strange building… not knowing which way to turn, and clinging to the arm of one of her adult daughters as if her life depended on it. I feel the beginnings of the heart stirring as I look at my dear mother's face and feel what she carried in her body for a lifetime. For a while mother and daughter are one… as I hold her, hold me and weep for the both of us. There is a sensing of this energy of feebleness going back up the female ancestral line, all the way back to that horrific moment in time when we first believed ourselves to be separate from God.

The beauty of the softened heart takes over my consciousness… a softness no separate individual can claim ownership of. It is the heart of all Being coming back for all its precious, unloved ones.

Will this character ever move quickly and smartly in the world… something that was always longed for? Goodness knows. And does it really matter? In the safety of the heart's cocoon, you realize you don't really mind.

And this landscape of vulnerability: will it need visiting again? I can't imagine not as inch by inch the Heart folds everything into itself.

The Great, Grand Noticer

October 8

Hold space for the "me," this construct, this character you call yourself. Hold space for all the crazy feeling energies that are bursting out of their prison of repression. So much floods in as we are being cracked open.

The sensations in the body make it all feel very real. It's not real. That's the glory of it; it's not real. Who you are is the Great, Grand Noticer of it all. Over time this Noticer starts to really wake up to itself, and the experience is not simply of observing (and we all know how faint that can feel at times), but also there are bursts of joy, waves of love and feelings of expansiveness and freedom. Gradually, eventually, the recognition that you are not the dream character, not the play, not the thoughts, feelings, sensations… it all takes firmer and firmer root, and you stand on new ground, as new ground, as original ground.

This is the only true happiness.

Fixing Your Life

October 10

The thought that something about you or your life needs fixing runs at an all-time high in most minds.

And it often marches in with a whole arsenal of feelings and upset behind it—all making it feel terribly convincing. This bundle of goodies has the whole force of separated consciousness behind it, and nearly the whole world would agree with you in a given moment that yes, you do need to do something about the whatever-it-is.

Over and over again you will be asked to sit tight in the face of this mental and emotional onslaught and to let Truth come in and "truth" these episodes of mind. Any part of you that is screaming "change, fix" is only another aspect of mind now dressed as all-knowing coach, spiritual teacher.

It's never about trying to change the dream character. You don't have a hope in hell at this stage of your evolution. The transformation of the personality takes place in its own natural, organic way when the winds of truth have held it, permeated it, so to speak.

So, keep holding the field of truth for all that blusters in out of the cold and wait and see what wants to happen. You are so not in charge of any of it.

Agitation and Space

November 2

It is possible to have fear coursing through the body and also to be aware of the spacious, all-is-wellness background of the moment.

It is very possible.

Don't let fear's rush of adrenaline fool you into believing that you are threatened in any way. When the rush of agitation is strong now, it is actually an affirmation that the space you are is large enough to hold it. Stand firm, hold steady as awareness, and see how every single wave of bodily sensation is just transient energy… popping in to say "Hello, am I welcome? Can I come home now? I'm so tired of being separate."

The marriage of presence and sensation, divinity and humanity, the loving mother with the baby in her arms… the prodigal son returning home… let it all come and finally find rest.

Pema and her younger daughter, Amaya

How Little We Know

December 7

Lying on one side in bed some time back, the movement came to turn over and lie on my back for a while. I was sure that was what I was going to do. As I went to turn, my body surprisingly turned all the way over to the other side… that just appearing as the most inviting position in the moment.

I thought what a perfect analogy that is for how little I know about where this life is going.

Mind thinks it knows something about our future. In truth, it doesn't have a clue. As the quickening of awakening takes place, we notice this more and more. We think X is going to happen. There is even sometimes a ring of synchronicity about it that convinces us of its rightness in the order of things. And then, lo and behold, it all changes on a dime and we are left dumbstruck, stranded in consciousness.

When this kind of experience cycles around enough times, you start to give up; the mind bows down in acknowledgment that something of real power and consequence has you in its embrace. This bowing down does not happen easily. We are brought to our sweet knees more often than we want to admit as this process unfolds.

Gradually the fear of not being in charge gives way to a great sense of relief. We don't have to do anything, know anything. Arriving freshly into each moment, we lay down our notions of control and rest in God's lap.

2010

The Dream Is Not Supposed to Be Good

January 14

It doesn't matter what is happening in your life. It doesn't matter at all. None of it matters. It is a dream… a dream of consciousness… that you are here to wake up out of.

The dream is not supposed to be good. It's based on separation—how can it be good? It's not called "samsara," the wheel of suffering, for nothing. Sure, there are wonderful moments of genuine love and connection; we have never fully left the Heart… but these are passing moments until the truth of us takes up residence.

We strive to make the dream of the ego better. It's a hopeless task. Sooner or later, something backfires again. Most of us are long enough in the tooth to see the futility of striving… and still we strive. Our minds can't help it.

This passage from *Cave in the Snow,* an account of the life of Tenzim Palmo, an amazing Englishwoman who retired to a cave in India for twelve years speaks directly to this. There was the occasion one spring when the thaw of the winter snows had begun and her cave was being systematically flooded.

The walls and the floor were getting wetter and wetter and for some reason I was also not very well. I was beginning to think, "Oh dear, what they say about caves is really true," and started to feel very down.

Suddenly the Buddha's First Noble Truth which she had learnt when she first encountered Buddhism struck her with renewed force. *I thought, "Why are you still looking for happiness in Samsara?" and my mind just changed around. It was like: That's right—Samsara is Dukka [the fundamental unsatisfactory nature of life]. It's OK that it's snowing. It's OK that I'm sick because that is the nature of Samsara. There's nothing to worry about. If it goes well, that's nice. If it doesn't go well, that's also nice. It doesn't make any difference. Although it sounds very elementary, at the time it was quite a breakthrough. Since then, I have never really cared about external circumstances.*

When things are off in my world of mind, I sometimes find it very helpful to remind myself, *Oh, yes, it's not supposed to be good, it's not supposed to be any different, it's just a dream… what is it that is eternally perfect and whole?* This can spark a feeling of relief, an internal standing up as the truth. The waves of mind about all that's wrong with my life and my body dissipate. Peace and lightness are restored. And all is well for another stretch.

When God Really Means Business with You

January 18

When God really means business with you, he takes you in his arms, and he whispers to you, and he says something like this:

It's time for you to come Home to me now, my love, so for the next whatever-it-takes, you're not going to be getting much of what you want in this world. And you're going to struggle and squirm and whimper and burn. And your beautiful heart will break over and over again. And finally, my beloved child, you will get sense, and you will lean back into me and realize this love is all that was ever wanted. And you and I will rejoice together as if there is no tomorrow.

Of course, the big problem is that you don't hear God's whispers, and you don't know he's holding you ever so close all the time.

Grounded by Love

January 21

The mind loves to make plans. It **LOVES** to make plans, to have a to-do list at the ready. It's a forward moving organism, a restless energy that is always looking towards the next thing, the next experience. Desire in motion. And it gets a lovely sense of accomplishment when "the next thing" is completed. And it might even rest for a bit in the peace of desirelessness, and then it's off seeking again.

It hates standstill, the feeling that it's going nowhere in life, that nothing is happening, nothing being accomplished. This is abhorrent for mind, and if standstill appears for some reason, a great feeling of pressure arises that you must do something. This pressure wants to coerce, cattle-prod, bulldoze you into movement.

This is a strategy of mind to move away from the discomfort of just resting. Sitting still, without the great distraction and entertainment of movement, could open a Pandora's box of uncomfortable feelings, a swirl of states that mind finds intolerable… perhaps loneliness, sadness, meaninglessness, anxiety.

As grace starts pulling the energy of mind home, you may well experience being grounded by Love. For some reason or another, you are not able to go out externally, do what you've always done. The usual distractions of mind are either not enticing or they are pulled away. You may well feel alarmed, very alarmed, wondering what the hell is happening to your life.

It is just the mind that is frightened. In truth, this is all great good news. All that's happening is that the uncomfortable energies, which the whole movement of your life has been built atop of, are being allowed to surface, and in so doing, they are being dissolved and released.

When these base energies can dissolve, you are no longer the hapless, programmed victim of them. The endless mind pursuit of distraction can stop, and true movement can arise, the movement of the heart.

It may be dark and difficult at times as this process is under way. Your will, what you know of as your personal will, is being coaxed into surrendering to the whole. There may not be many people in your life who will understand you, and this is part of the arduousness and loneliness of this journey.

What finally emerges from the ashes is the aroma of joy, agenda free movement and the soft glow of the opened Heart.

Don't Be Afraid of the Silence

January 27

Don't be afraid of the silence. It's what you are. How weird that we are scared of our own Self.

What would have to be given up to rest as ourselves? The cacophony of thought, pots and pans of thoughts clanging together, all of it totally, equally rubbish. There are no words befitting the magnitude of how useless, how meaningless all the thinking is. It is utterly, unequivocally USELESS.

We believe it is our thinking that directs the life, that moves us, makes decisions. That is just another lie. Have you noticed how often the body moves to do something without any prior thought? A nose gets scratched, a yawn happens, a blanket gets wrapped more tightly around you. What is it that does that… goodness knows, but it is obviously not thought.

It is so with everything. You do not need thinking to live your life. You can relax deeply, deeply.

Don't be afraid of the silence. It is just the mind that is scared… some fear appearing in the quiet spaciousness of You. Hang out there with this fear. It's a good "healthy" fear to sit with.

And a Little Child Shall Lead Them

January 30

Have mercy on the one who leaves to go outside you seeking love, approval. Have the greatest of mercy for her. If she knew a better way, God knows she'd be doing it.

What other way did she learn as a child but to try to please… or whatever the particular survival strategy was? *I will please them, and then they will love me, and I can belong here, and I will be OK.* How basic, how primal is this—the destiny of every human being growing up in a world of conditional love.

Making her wrong serves nothing and just continues the harshness, an internal harshness that becomes more and more intolerable to a heart that's being tenderized.

How smart is this little one, how incredibly smart and true she is, that every instinct in her would go toward what she knows to be the only thing that would save her… Love. That what she seeks outside herself will not be found is just evidence of how the mind's misguided, thwarted projections of separation can never find completion.

Her homing instincts are faultless. Deep in the recesses of her beingness she knows she is Love itself… she is Love that can rest only in Love. Honor her with all your might. Every one of her failures in finding love outside her is your gift. Hold her to you until the raw wounding of the heart is soothed, and the great ache of separation is done.

And our gratitude flows for how this painful dream of lack and specialness becomes a right royal display of Love seeing itself everywhere.

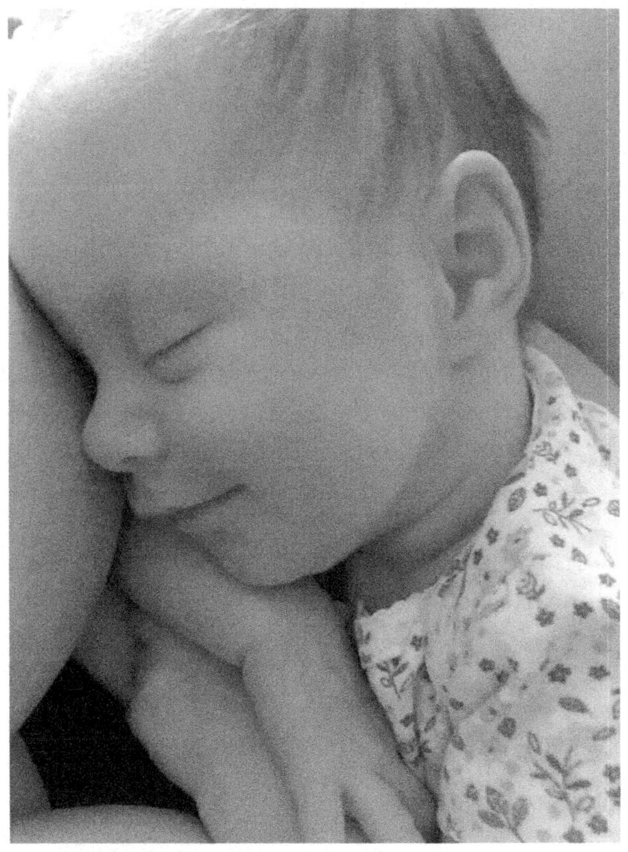

Who Is It That Needs the Loving?

February 2

We cry out that we want to love. We long to be love in every cell. We wonder why we can't love a certain person or whatever number of people there are floating outside our sphere of affection. We are so intent on figuring out what stands in the way of our loving someone. The mind can get super engaged with this and just create more angst.

It is to remember that our dear minds cannot resolve this stuff. It is an organic process of the heart, and the walls between you and the unlovable ones will crumble in their own time. You can be assured of this. What is really helpful is a gentle turning back to yourself and offering of compassion to this part of you that is suffering and that cannot love yet. This is what gets skipped over in our eagerness to love the world.

You are unable to love because of particular conditioning that you are carrying, some pool of ancestral energy you sit in, some aspect of your karmic totality. Your projections and judgments are totally innocent, beyond your control in the moment. They just arise in the mind, no one responsible for them. Impersonal turbulence.

Bringing kindness, patience and understanding to our own closed-heart-of the-moment, when we can… this is the key to our overall heart opening.

Sparks

February 15

Keep meeting the nothingness of the ego until it melts into the Nothingness of God.

When freedom from egoic consciousness is what your life is devoted to… don't be surprised when it doesn't always feel like a romp in the park.

Don't raise your head as an egoic anything. Keep it bowed down, as close to the ground as possible. It will rise naturally when it has been emptied out of all fanciful imaginings of specialness.

Devote yourself to the unknown. Give yourself into its custody, right there in your own heart, and bear the ride.

It is in the fire of not being able to fix the personal self that the woundedness and repressed energies inherent in that woundedness can make themselves known. And little by little, the cleansing happens, and the heart is forced open to our own beautiful Self.

The ego mind is reduced over and over and over again to nothing. Every place where it thinks it is a *somebody* or *something* has something to offer, has a rosy enlightened future… each and every place whacked. This journey is the deepest humbling.

It is inconceivable to the mind that there could be love or security outside of what is familiar to it in external forms.

Stepping out of the "should, have to, need to" is a great act of kindness to yourself. It is an act of aliveness.

What is the resurrection of Christ, the resurrection of You? Only thought not believed.

Child of Unworthiness

February 20

This prayer/poem is dedicated to all of us healing from the original loss of love. Gratefully, the Heart wins through and calls all of us who believed ourselves to be unlovable back into its ever open, waiting arms.

Child of Unworthiness

Dear child of unworthiness
Let me hold you close for what may be these last few times
Caress your sweet face, your precious limbs
These holy limbs of God

How can I say goodbye to you, my love
My closest one
You have lived in the marrow of these bones

You have given me a life
A hunchback of a life
The perfect life for freedom's call

A harsh and merciless land of less than, better than
Of grinding, grating thought with no reprieve
Where sister becomes enemy in the flash of a stinging thought
My brother's suffering pursued in the cruel hope of relieving my own

Dear Father God, Beloved Heart
It is only to You that I can bring this child
Take her home now, her great work is done
She has brought me unerringly to your shores

Pardon her, dear Father, for ever believing she was anything
other than your own precious child
Bury her in the voluminous folds of your merciful, bountiful heart
May she rest here now forevermore
Dissolved, adored and free… at last.

As Good as It Gets

February 23

I find it a helpful spiritual practice to remind myself at moments that "this is as good as it gets." The mind is a movement of energy out—out to thought, to experience, to desires, to fears.

"This is as good as it gets" is a stopper. It can for a brief spell stop the movement of attention out and land you just here. Just here. No next moment. Nothing better than this. Nothing needing to be better, nicer than this. No place to arrive at. It bypasses all the unresolved issues, material of your life, futurized yearnings. "As good as it gets" includes what's here, any sensations, any brokenness of body, just includes it without any thoughts about it.

Let it all end here. Let all the striving for betterness come to rest in this "nothing going on." Nothing happening. NOTHING happening.

Sparks Two

February 26

How cold and perfunctory everything seems outside the soft glow of the Heart.

God's heart is not touched by our fancy robes of arrogance. God's heart loves the dress, the overcoat of humility.

The mind is unruly and loves to roam. Put it on a leash. Rein it in so you can actually see what it's up to.

You are the master and the master comforter. Where else can this body-mind content rest? Only in You. There is no other resting ground around.

There is nothing out there for you in the external world. Nothing. Just crumbs. Crumbs of approval.

Give the mind permission to think whatever it thinks. It's going to do that, anyways. Don't recoil from the harsh thoughts. See them and know they arise from a hurting place, from a hurting one. This one needs love.

Be tender with your sweet body, this body that bears so much for you. It shelters all the pain and discomfort of a separated being, and it is your precious vehicle as you journey to freedom.

We were taught to trust so few of our natural movements. Only what was acceptable in our family and environment.

The unworthiness and inferiority we feel at times is just too painful to hang out with, so the mind desperately tries to find places where you are "better than" the ones you feel to be "less than." Come back. Don't listen to the mind as it tries to resurrect a "better than." This stuff goes nowhere. Come back to the pain in the body, to the distressed one, and ask for Love to pour through into this one.

Loving Yourself as the Conditioned "Me"

March 5

We are all deeply challenged in the arena of self-love. We can be easier on ourselves when we start to really take in that this ego-construct that we believe ourselves to be is absolutely flawed. Everyone's ego-construct is flawed. The ego arises as a thought of separation, of lack, of not-whole, so to expect your body-mind to be content and happy with itself is actually madness. It is all the opposite. It is most often in conflict with itself, carrying oodles of self-hatred.

So, it's to take a look at this body-mind of yours… there are so many aspects of it that appear to be unlovable and hateful. It's designed that way. One part of the mind hating another part of the mind, that's all that's ever going on… and EVERY MIND is equally intolerable of itself; that's the nature of mind. We are one mind. So everyone has a core story that will feel absolutely unlovable. Either you're convinced you're "bad," "ugly," "weird," "crazy," "stupid," "useless," "unlovable"—or fill in whatever it is for you.

Whatever this is, this is what you have come here to love.

This core story of unlovability that we all carry, in whichever form it shows up for us—**this is what binds us most deeply to the belief that we exist as a separate, personal self.** This is why we are graced to come to see and dislodge our core patterning. It is also the end of the suffering.

This unpacking is not easy because of the contracted energy that holds these beliefs in place. These beliefs, following our karmic imprint, were sustained through experiences with others where we did not feel loved. For the tender, exquisitely sensitive energy body of the baby, this is taken in as deeply painful. The nervous system of the child is not equipped to handle this, and so it must be pushed down out of conscious awareness as unintegrated molecules of energy.

At the same time as the pain is repressed, the beliefs are being set in place, and walls of protection get erected around the heart. From there on, life is lived in such a way as to avoid ever touching that pain again.

We may be able to live a good part of our lives without engaging with the pain, but we live handicapped lives of disconnect, of micro-macro managing our environment. This is ultimately exhausting, and something finally wants to crack open.

When the willingness is in place, life starts to orchestrate itself to bring attention to what has been buried. The pain of believing you are not lovable, not good enough, starts to get squeezed to the surface.

Simply allowing this pain to emerge is all that is needed. Anything else, as in the voice of reason from yourself or other, is trying to put a band-aid over a festering wound. It does not land in the child-self's being. This is why affirmations, spiritual concepts, non-dual language cannot do the deeper healing. They cannot penetrate the walls around the heart. They are like mental arrows storming the castle walls of the ego-mind that just bounce back because these walls are comprised of energy. This energy can only melt by being fully felt and experienced, more often than not in the sweet release of long held-in tears. If it is felt as a grip of sensation in the body, it will dissolve gradually when held in awareness. Love is the greatest dissolving agent for this pain energy, your own compassion or that of another, which ultimately is your own reflected back to you.

This cleansing and purging breaks the trance of the mind and allows the true, natural strength of your being to come forth. What emerges gradually, gratefully, as the layers of mind are washed away, is a natural knowing that you are deeply loved, that you are Love itself.

Pioneers of the Heart

March23

We are pioneers of the heart. We are being called to meet and hold with the heart of a mother all that could not be met before, all of our karmic totality. We are not talking clean, pretty, ordered, Academy-Award lives here. Much of the time we're talking mess.

We are talking the mess of all the disowned parts of us—the ones that are now crawling out of the dark caves of egoic consciousness. It's as if the news has reached them that they can come Home now. Out they come, the awkward, shamed ones covered in self-consciousness, the hopeless ones, the needy ones, the ones that don't even have a name, that show up as confusing emotional, energetic storms, as burning, malaise, exhaustion in the body.

At some point we are graced to be able to sit beside and hold the hand of each and every one of them, each and every wave of mind. We say "I love you. Thank you for coming to be freed, to free me." We gradually learn not to twist and turn and try to squirm away from what is present in our bodies. We hold steadfast as the heart, as the space of truth, keeping it all company, hanging out with what has never known love, what is aching for love and permission to be.

It is without doubt the hardest, most intense work we will ever be asked to do, but it's what we came here for. It is our glorious Homecoming.

Sparks Three

April 9

Tenderness is an exquisite form of self-inquiry. It dismantles the walls and armoring of the ego construct in the most beautiful way.

Come into full contact with what's here. Stop fleeing the body.

There are times to be the solid stance of Truth and not follow one thought of your story, and there are times you enter fully into the center of the story, into the eye of the storm.

Mind has created the most intricate, complex web of an illusional universe of energy appearing real. One thought, one flurry of thought believed, and we are back in the grip of the web.

The mind thrives on secrecy, on privacy. Expose the mind. Let it out to play and to be seen.

Your relationship with the ego-child is to love it and to free it.

The ego's drive, deep at the heart of all its other desires and shenanigans is to be special, to stand out from the whole. And it doesn't mind which way this gets accomplished… whether you are the most superior one or the most inferior one. The happiest one or the most miserable one. This is not to call the ego a bad guy… it is simply to see that the momentum of energy arises from a thought of separation, and it must be held up at any cost.

Often, we long for a voice of compassion to speak to us tenderly and say, "Tell me what ails you, my love." Be this for yourself. Let the wounded heart cry out all its woes, all the things that are wrong with you and your life. You are your own true love.

Everything is coming to you to engage with your heart. It's not satisfied with anything less than your full heart. It will come in various forms to you until there is no opposition, no bracing against, no warding off—an all-inclusive embracing.

Self-Inquiry and Emotionally Charged Memories

April 14

This is a lovely piece from the Irish spiritual teacher, Jac O'Keeffe… the simplicity of making these "child-states" safe:

We're changing the feeling around the memories. Memories are fine. They're not a problem. If they have an emotional charge, an emotional rush, it's going to take an awful lot of "Who's the one having the thought, who's the one having the feeling?" You could be doing that for three years. Or you can go in (into the mind) for three minutes, deal with it and get out.

If you go in, and you see a scene where that original pain happened, if you imagine yourself going to that young fellow, and just holding *him* and loving *him* and giving him a safe place… *it changes the memory. It's like energetically something goes back in time and it resolves the original package so the resource cupboard of your memories have a different set of ingredients.*

You walk into the scene and make it safe. ***MAKE IT SAFE.*** *And energetically you're placing a different energy in the part of your brain that has that memory which runs to adrenaline, or fear, or shame, or guilt, or whatever the rush is. It's just an energy thing. Mind is just energy; we can break it all down to energy work.*

Transmuting Pain into Love

April 21

Let the tight, painful sensations in the body be nestled here into this Body of Presence.

Let them burrow down, find their comfiest spot in this womb of Love.

Let them have their full time in utero, however long they need to come to completion.

Lifetimes they have waited for the grace to even come into conscious awareness. This is their glorious birthing, and Love has its own timing with them now.

And this is a Love that never calls for anything to go away, that knows nothing of faster or better. Quiet and steady and open. Receiving and tenderizing all that is being birthed into it.

Killing Myself Softly with My Song

April 30

Oh… this song of conditioning, this song of "me and my and mine," this endless karmic melody. How strong is its voice, how captivating its refrain. It hammers out the thoughts, churns up the emotions, fills the body with its grip.

And it kills us. Deadens us. Cements us into blocks of paralysis. Or moves us in an exhausting dance to the tunes and whims of untruth.

Could it be the time to stop singing? To stop reciting the mantras of childhood, the mantras of a totally unfixable, separated one?

Or could it EVER be the time to stop making the song "mine"? To not let one note, false or true, be yours. To let the band play on, minus you. Just notes and phrases spinning through space.

Ah… the blessed relief of even a short spell of "nobody home."

Wee Notions of Specialness

June 7

I often notice the rush of pleasure that arises in my mind when I do someone a favor, and I imagine they're going to be pleased with me, or when I fantasize on some future incident where my ego will be stroked in some way. I call it the rush of specialness.

For some time, I used to recoil against this feeling, seeing it as so egoic, not spiritual, not of the heart. And I even thought the recoiling itself was the mark of more spiritual maturity. The recoiling is just the ego condemning itself. This leaves the box of the mind intact, just continuing to do its merry dance, uninterrupted.

Recently I have been seeing how sweet it is to notice these rushes of specialness and just to see the innocence of them—this character believing there is someone here doing something, something that will earn it some approval, belonging, connection, validation. It is just the ego's misguided search for love, and how harmless, how beautiful is this really.

Seeing the innocence is the opening of the heart, and you notice how this waft of love kind of encircles the mind, blessing it, holding it. Nothing else needed, indeed.

The Known and the Fear of the Unknown

June 20

The I-mind feels safe in the known, in thought. The nature of the thoughts has no relevance. Good happy thoughts, painful stinging thoughts—all the same. This is what it knows. This is its home.

It is terrified of anything outside thought.

Because of its fear, it thinks there's this huge dropping into the unknown, into spaciousness/vastness that has to happen. It fears it will disappear in the space and be annihilated.

But the spaciousness is right there, all around, all the time. The thoughts are simply appearing, arising in It. The I-mind is surrounded by and held in the safety of stillness, always.

At times the I-mind may make these exhortations: "Take me into the unknown," as if it is this amazing feat that has to happen. This is again just another thought.

It thinks it's encased in something that's binding it. It's not. The spaciousness is just right here, to be experienced in any moment.

If you watch the mind, you will see how it's kind of desperate to name, explain, categorize, report what's going on with its thinking, its process. When it can label something, it feels a little safer, more relaxed, on firmer ground. It hates stuff going on that it cannot interpret.

We are here to get real comfy with the unknown, to recognize it as the only real safety, to see it as Home. The unknown is our Home.

The Beloved's Hands

August 9

The unloved corners of our being wait. If there were any purpose to time, it would be this: the time it takes for the Beloved to reveal what you have not yet been able to love, the time it takes for the Beloved to soften your heart through the relentless pain and longing of being human.

As Love moves in, we learn to let this dear character called "me" do what it does. To take our mental hands off it and to lay on it a different pair of hands. More natural hands.

Hands from your heart that bless and stroke and speak approving words of "okayness." Hands that fold your human body into their embrace. Not just the sweet, imagined body of your inner child but the broken, mind-battered body of an older being, no longer so agile or worldly beautiful.

Hands that love to love whatever they hold… that are drawn irresistibly to the object of their secret devotion—you, just as you are, with your hidden little idiosyncrasies and shamings, your hits and buzzes of arrogance, your compulsions and so-called flaws: All so *nothing* in this tender flow.

Hands that bring only mercy and benevolence, that whisper and will whisper to our dying day: "Come and lay with me. Come, lay here forever with me, my dear, dear, sweet child."

The Great Stripping

August 12

Thank you, dear Father God, Beloved Heart for never giving up on me. For prying my grasping hands off the shiny jewels of approval and specialness, the cherished heirlooms of lack, of *less than, better than.*

The precious pearls of holy insights and concepts understood that make me dream more deeply that I am someone of note.

You come with fervor to take them all. You leave me naked without my costume jewelry, my many baubles of mind.

You would dress me only in your one unchanging garment of Truth.

And your ruthless uncaring of whatever it takes for this child to stand again as only yours. This, at last, I come to see as Love's deepest caring. And what remains then, alone, unbidden, on these lips, but one undying thank you.

2011

The Beloved Walks Beside You

March 5

The Beloved walks beside you. Always. She offers to you, as this beautiful organism of name and form, a very tender, gentle sense of accompaniment, meeting your pace of walking, breathing, and embracing your every activity with a loving, all-accepting presence.

Love loves everything in its path in equal measure, caring naught for rich or poor, plump or lean, productive or not. All the dualistic extremes that the ego worships and identifies so fiercely with, all dissolve into nothing in this tender flow.

Love is light. It is not laden with sentiment. It folds, curls around all it meets in a soft embrace, never intruding, picking apart, analyzing,

Let the Beloved walk beside you. Let the awareness of there being "two of you" be here, you as the personality/body and You as this loving, great mother presence. Allow the small you to be like an invalid at times, fragile, vulnerable. Indeed, this journey home is strewn with visitations of vulnerability. Let the Beloved walk you to the bathroom, take you through your day, smoothing out the creases, simply adoring you, your humanness and your precious little personal ways of being.

For You are this Love. This Great Mother Love. And the dream character of this small you can gradually hunker down, nestle into and dissolve into You, this great soft belly of Love.

It'll Be Better When...

March 8

What an incredible amount of striving goes on in this world. We all have this perpetual carrot dangling right in front of our eyes with its seductive mantra of "It'll be better when…"

It'll be better when… when I'm awake, when I come out of stagnation, when my heart is more open, when my body feels better. Not to mention the all-time compelling desires: finding your true purpose or a spiritual partner.

These futurized yearnings are all the same. One is as good as another to fulfill the one purpose they share: to keep you in the loop and maze of the mind, by convincing you that happiness lies in something being different in the dream. Happiness does not reside in anything changing about you or your life situation. It is a dream after all.

Freedom lies only in waking up right out of the mirage—a force of truth that emerges, stands erect like a pillar of light, a mountain, that dismisses all conditioned thought and energetic pulls for the untruths they are, the smoke and mirrors of illusion.

"It'll be better when…" What an awful joke we play on ourselves.

Even the desire to realize the Self, as right and fitting as it may seem, is still just another desire and keeps your attention in the realm of mind. It's just a brighter colored, more succulent carrot. But a carrot, no matter how appealingly it's dangled, is just a carrot.

The Self is Absolute. It is nameless, formless, dreamless, imageless, divinity.

It is just This. It is nothing happening, no sense of anything. It is pristine stillness and perfect peace.

Let Pain Rest Now

March 17

Let pain rest now in the lap of your being.

Hold it steady with arms that know the rightness of its hereness.

Old it is, as old as time, compacted molecules of all things separate.

Warmth and refuge it seeks, having traveled far from the frozen wastelands of ignorance, denial and repression.

Let it come home now, no more to ache in cold and disconnect.

Let it melt in the flow of long-held tears, in the warmth and glow of a softening heart.

Making way for all things good, for compassion and kindness and humility.

Making way to walk in the world with the Beloved as your very own heart.

Celebration or Compassion

March 19

There are times when you can actually celebrate the presence of tight energy and contraction in the body. A celebratory feeling naturally arises in the relief of recognizing that it means nothing, means zilch about you. It is just energy appearing in the field of consciousness that You are. What You are cannot be touched, tampered with, affected in any way by anything happening in consciousness.

This is not an abandonment of yourself. It is true seeing.

There are other times when the tenderness of the heart is called on and is the most natural response to pain. These times it is a sweet relief to let the pain cry itself out, to say "Hello, welcome" to old feelings, bound energies that are just now coming to the light of day.

One way is not more correct than another. It is always simply whatever is happening, how you are moved in the moment to greet old conditioning or energies in the body. Sometimes compassion arises; sometimes the more absolutist seeing is the way.

The mind can kick up a storm of thinking in wondering what is the best way to be with pain. *Am I supposed to open my heart to this or is it better just not to believe it?* These questions always seem so valid in the moment, but it is just more of the same old regular mind play. The sophistication of the thinking kind of obscures the fact that it is just more meaningless thought.

Don't pay attention to it; come back and notice what is actually happening, and let the natural discernment of your own truth lead the way.

Sparks Four

April 15

It was a grand day for me when I came to be able to sit with pain in my solar plexus and not follow the thoughts and story about it and to see that sitting with the sensation in my body actually felt easier than believing all the tortured thoughts. The suffering is indeed the labeling and the story.

How imperfect your life situation is is exactly how PERFECT it is. The personal will is broken down, not by having an

Academy Award life but rather by the ego not getting what it wants. Take heart and know that everything is being exquisitely orchestrated for you by the Divine Hand whose only interest is the humbling of your will and your return to Love.

This big phenomenal whirl of energy that we call the world: if we look for ourselves in a scrap of this, we are lost, spinning wheels in this mad cyclone of time. Come back, come back to the timeless nothingness over and over again, until it is known that You are This, and This is You.

Be still, my love, in preparation for your Homecoming.

Good Friday, Good Life

April 22

We are all being crucified in our own way. Love places us in this crucible called our life, and everything that is not of the Holy is consumed: our arrogance, our smallness, our knots of self-consciousness, our wounds, our intimate hopes and desires. All that upholds the lie of "me."

When the Beloved as Fire Master is done, we emerge humbled, yielding, soft-eyed, without issue or future, and free at last to play in the fields of the Lord.

A Few More Sparks

May 10

Wherever the shaky, insecure ego has been triggered, expect it to be triggered in that same arena many times over until you can stand undisturbed in the face of what was always a catalyst for pain. Heralding the end of all suffering.

Even with years and years of doing awareness work, I was never able to just stand as the truth and not believe the mind. There was and is still too much of a tug from the emotion and energetics in the body. I find the more this energy gets broken up, the lighter it all feels and there is a natural and greater ability then to just dismiss the mind as illusion and imagination.

Compassion for the Conditioning

May 11

How sweet and freeing it feels to love your own character, the conditioned "me," even when, *especially* when, it is acting out of woundedness, desire and any form of separation patterning. A blessed ending to all things wrong with us.

And what a great practice it is to see how gentle and understanding we can be with ourselves in that particular challenging arena of the body—when the character doesn't do what's called "best" for the body. Not eating "right" and exercising "enough" must fall into the relieving embrace of surrender and non-doership, just like all things human.

Mid-May Sparks

May 16

The body, until it is filled with light, is a repository for the pain of separation. We are gradually graced to meet the energetics in the body as feeling, as sensation, meeting it with gentleness and compassion. This breaks the trance of mind, and we come to stand anew on original ground… *as* original ground.

Compassion for yourself breaks through when this happens.

You can't willpower the heart to open. Just rest in the knowing of your true intention and willingness, and in some unexpected moment you will be surprised by a tender, organic movement of the Heart.

As chaotic as the mind is, it's about getting to know the bare bones of it intimately. We all have one or two core stories on which most of the mind activity hinges. We can become masters at spotting the most subtle connections and threads to these. Eventually it all gets seen through as the great lie that it is.

There Is Nobody Here

May 18

In 2008, I visited the Peruvian jungle for a series of deep shamanic journeys.

On one of these journeys the truth of existence was irrevocably seen: that in the entirety of this place we call the universe, THERE IS NOBODY HERE. That nothing ever happened, nothing is happening, and nothing will ever happen. That we are all playing charades, parlor games at their best… pretending we are "somebodies." That there is nothing outside the vibrant, shining stillness of the Absolute. Words could never capture how riveting this seeing was and how utterly shocking it was to the mind.

And the truth is shocking to the mind that believes so completely in its own existence.

Spiritual Concepts and a Deeper Healing

May 20

Spiritual concepts and non-dual language cannot do the deeper healing. They cannot penetrate the protective walls around the heart. They are like mental arrows storming the castle walls of the ego-mind that just bounce back because these walls are comprised of energy.

This energy can only melt by being fully felt and experienced, more often than not in the sweet release of long held-in tears. If it is felt as a grip of sensation in the body, it will dissolve gradually when held in awareness. Love is the greatest dissolving agent for this pain energy, your own compassion or that of another, which ultimately is your own reflected back to you.

This cleansing and purging break the trance of the mind and allow the true natural strength of your being to come forth. What emerges gradually, gratefully, as the layers of mind are washed away, is a natural knowing that you are deeply loved, that you are Love itself.

Unpacking the Core Story

May 22

Before we can truly know there is nobody here, we will visit and revisit our core story of unlovability in whichever way it shows up for us. This is what binds us most deeply to the belief that we exist as a separate, personal self.

The unpacking of this lynchpin is not easy because of the contracted energy that holds these beliefs in place. These beliefs, following our karmic imprint, were sustained through experiences with others where we did not feel loved. For the tender, exquisitely sensitive energy body of the baby, this is taken in as deeply painful. The nervous system of the child is not equipped to handle this, and so it must be pushed down out of conscious awareness as unintegrated molecules of energy.

At the same time as the pain is repressed, the beliefs are being set in place, and walls of protection get erected around the heart. From there on, life is lived in such a way as to avoid ever touching that pain again.

When the willingness is in place, life starts to orchestrate itself to bring attention to what has been buried. The pain of believing you are not lovable, not good enough, starts to get squeezed to the surface.

Simply allowing this pain to emerge is all that is needed. Anything else, as in the voice of reason from yourself or other, is trying to put a band-aid over a festering wound. It does not land in the child-self's being.

Meeting Ourselves in the Body

May 25

Not leaving the body and staying with the painful, uninterpretable sensations, burning and malaise that can arise in this process of embodiment is about the hardest thing we are asked to do. Holding space for the impulses that come to "do" something to distract from it, anything rather than just keep it company… this is the work of warriors.

Reminding ourselves of what is truly going on here can bring greater acceptance and openness. We are meeting the past in the body—our own past, our parents' past, the somatic and emotional history of our ancestors. We are clearing out, transmuting the pain of separation.

Take heart in knowing that there is no work more valuable than this. Nothing could be more important than facing the pain we have spent lifetimes avoiding. Nothing will ultimately bring greater joy.

The marriage of presence and sensation, divinity and humanity, the loving mother with the baby in her arms… the prodigal son returning home… let it all come and finally find rest.

This sacred union that takes us beyond all notions of union.

Waking Up to Love

May 29

For some of us who have an easier ability to access space and presence, we must be cautious that this is not used as a means of avoiding meeting the pain of separation.

The walls of the ego can remain intact in this way… it's like the ego remains as a bubble in the space. The Love that we are cannot be felt and truly flow in a sustained way through these forms until the ego walls are ruptured and dissolved.

This happens when our true human vulnerability and frailty is felt, and the ego bows down to the Beloved. This process of humbling is the most challenging part of true awakening but it becomes the most tender, sweetest place on earth as these dear hearts and bodies of ours break over and over and over again until they are filled with light.

And there remains only gratitude to the Beloved for stirring the embers of our hearts into its own eternal blaze.

Child of the Lie

June 16

I come for you now
Child of the lie

Laden no longer with sentiment
Or need to linger at childhood's favorite wounds

Enough of lives, of layers, of nebulous energies
I want you to know the lie

The flat out lie that you are
Anything other than Life Itself

I want to find the very core of you
And wrap it in a love so thick and binding

That not one vestige of unlovedness
Could ever rise again to mar
The beauty of my sister's face

Or hunt for love in a world
Whose lonely halls were never built for such

Into the belly of mother I go
On a mission of love

Through the waters of separation
The tiny folds of fetus flesh
Bone and cell and synapse

But where is the center?
Is it the heart, the gut

Some molecules of life
Sourcing into human form?

I wait, perplexed, to know

And then, somehow, unannounced
Wisps of air
The softest nothing
A gentle breeze of Love

No child, no lie, no core, no me
Nothing to meet, or heal or hold
A Love complete unto itself

A hint of a smile if a breeze can smile
Benevolent nod, a faint murmuring

Yes, my love, all that dust
And always, only, ever This.

The Beauty of Burning

June 17

How challenging is the burning away and deconstruction of the ego. How deeply challenging and how incredibly beautiful.

These dear, repressed energies, long held in parts that have never seen the light of day walking out again in the sunshine of our hearts. Explanatory words like "transmutation" and "waking up" fade away and there is only the poignancy, the sweetness, the joy of the Heart that we are, calling, calling, receiving, loving, stroking, reclaiming. All our yearning and longing finally finding completion in what sourced it all along… Love, pure Love.

May we live for this and this alone. May we make the dangerous prayer to the Beloved that knows the way. May these sweet heads of ours bow and bow and bow again until the Bow is one glorious prostration of Self to Self, of Love to Love… and only Love.

Find a Hand to Hold

June 19

Find a hand to hold.

Be vulnerable.

Speak what you don't want to speak, but you really do want to speak.

Shining through our soft vulnerability is the enormous backbone of the Self.

Being Vulnerable

June 24

We usually have a lot of fear about being vulnerable. We probably got ridiculed as a child, or at least the tender parts of us were never met with love and understanding, so we shut down, and an unconscious decision got made that we'd never expose ourselves like that again. Parts of us became frozen and numb.

The melting of these energies and walls around the heart is very tender, delicate work, and the energy itself knows when it is safe to come forth. In fact, it has an exquisite radar system for knowing with whom safety lies. You don't even have to know yourself if you trust a particular space; the child energy will know.

There is great sweetness and relief as each layer of frozen energy melts. It is the opening of the heart; it is true intimacy with ourselves and others, and it is the gateway into the Heart of God.

The Work of the Heart

June 27

As the sense of spaciousness grows and we delve more deeply into the work of the heart, we are asked to meet more intense energies than we are accustomed to. Old pain from suppressed parts of the psyche start seeping out of our bodies in what is often referred to as a purging or cleansing.

It may surface as physical pain or, as is very often the case, as mental/emotional pain. Our sense of specialness gets chipped away at. Some triggering happens, and in no time, we feel consumed in a heavy energy that fills up the whole screen of our consciousness. It is helpful to remember that a big chunk of old ego pain energy is coming through… coming OUT of our system. It is necessary… it is OK… it is the way of it. It feels so personal, but there's nothing personal about it. It is just collective pain energy. It wraps itself around that personal self with a suffocating fierceness, and there is only despair and hopelessness about what a terrible person you are. It will always revolve around the small me—that's the way it gets its grip. That's the way the pain is felt.

See if you can rise above the awful thinking and relate directly to the pain in a way that would be natural for you with a small hurting child… "I know you need to come. I know it's so hard for you. I know you've been trapped in here forever, and I wish I could welcome you a little more. I love you. I'm sorry. Thank you for coming at last."

Energy is just like a person, it knows when it is being resisted, it knows when it is being received. The more you can hold the consciousness of welcoming and understanding, the easier it can be for it to move through. Waves of tears may come and go. They are freeing you, and they have their own heart-softening beauty.

Do whatever you can to be gentle and to hold the bigger picture that it is your freedom that's happening. And this work you are doing has a far greater impact than you can know of in the moment. It is serving your family, your ancestors and coming generations.

In time, the more these old energies get broken up, and their gravitational force is diminished, the lighter it all feels, and there is a natural and greater ability then to just dismiss the mind as illusion and imagination. And what incredible grace this is.

This Is Your Dream

July 5

Everything you see and hear and feel is coming FROM you; it is not coming TO you.

All the vignettes, situations, appearances are projections ballooned out from your own unconscious mind. It is your DREAM. Your unconscious is the author of your dream.

And it serves you well. Without it and all the dream figures in it that disturb you, you would never know what is not yet free. This is the great gift of your life.

A Storyless Meeting

July 9

As Love pours itself more expansively into the body-mind structure, deeper layers of ego are exposed for dissolution. Triggers happen to the personal self, more intensely than may have been known before. The first response is often at the mental level where a rush of distressed thinking starts up.

As much as is humanly possible, we want to come down below the level of thought and meet the pain energy where it is originating in the body.

The pain of separation is stored in the body. When it is not met here as sensation, it rises up into the emotional body and if it cannot be felt there, it continues on up to the mental realm and results in all the obsessive thinking that is familiar to us.

The ego is wired, through the strategies of projection and repression, to not feel pain at its source—in the body. This is how its continued existence is assured: all the attention is maintained in the madness of thinking where resolution can never be found.

The practice of siphoning our attention back down from thought to where the body is in a grip and holding this in Presence—this is the most direct way of meeting ourselves. Opening our hearts to what is alive in the body. And much to our surprise, we find that this storyless meeting with pain is actually not painful. It is just sensation. Truly it is the thoughts that create the suffering.

This ongoing meeting of separation energy with Presence is the beginning of the end of you. This grace-filled alchemy softens our edges, dissolves the hard shell of the ego and awakens the Quan Yin of the heart, where all it wants is to bring refuge to the untold pain of the collective prodigal son.

The bad dream of the ego becomes a love dream of the heart.

Surrender

July 11

Love will not and cannot give you what you want. This would just maintain the travesty of recycled existence in time and space. But Love, in its deepest caring, will give you everything you need to break down the personal will and take you Home.

You are being reclaimed by Love. Tarry not in boarding the only ship that leaves the dock of the ego. It's called "Surrender." The sails are hoisted; the band plays its holy mix of longing and celebration. And there is only one destination now. Home, sweet Home. Love, pure Love.

The Meaninglessness of All Thought

July 16

Some years back, I had a series of deep shamanic journeys in the Amazon jungle. Many truths were revealed in these, heralding what would in time be fully known and lived in everyday existence.

In one of these opening experiences, the mind fell away, and there was just this large, spacious Nothing. Just NOTHING, NOTHING, NOTHING. No Ramana, no Jesus, no me, no nobody. Just THIS. Alive Stillness.

And these offshoots into mind appeared. Like arrows of thought darting up out of nowhere. And they were seen to be nothing, to have no meaning whatsoever. Thought has no meaning. It is all rubbish. Absolute rubbish. In the seeing of this, there was another small play of thought about the greatness of what was being seen and then the "I" thought of how great I was to be seeing this.

There was an immediate thud of guilt and contraction and condemnation of this ego arrogance.

And then, to my great shock, it was known that all this guilt about the arrogant "me" was also all nothing, absolutely nothing. Of no greater import than the thought, "it's raining." Of no import whatsoever. Rubbish.

All the guilt of lifetimes for nothing. There are no words befitting the magnitude of how useless and meaningless all this guilt and self-attack is.

In regular life, I used to think it was spiritually noble to catch egoic arrogance and feel bad about it. See it, notice it, yes. But self-condemnation leads nowhere but to unnecessary suffering.

And it all plays itself out for each of us. The dance does its dance until it is all seen through as this remarkable but unremarkable display of phenomenal energy.

As Energy Comes Home

July 30

Compacted, frozen pain energy is like a baby. As a mother does not address her fussing baby with nondual language, neither do we in the meeting with ourselves. You may know and understand a lot and be conscious, but these energies are not conscious.

You come into direct relationship with them. Direct but gentle, not piercing, not intrusive, not willpowering anything. Asking contracted energy what it needs is a lovely way of acknowledging its presence and becoming intimate with it. Everything that is not at rest wants to be acknowledged, to be received and bathed in gentleness and benevolence.

It calls for a major slowing down, to receive the old, repressed cries of pain that show up now as contractions, as bodily sensations.

The mind is conditioned to want results—the result in this case being the disappearance of the disturbance. It is very, very sweet to bypass this, allowing the body to have what it has for as long as it does. You may walk around for hours with disturbance but you can be nurturing and aware of your precious cargo. Mercy and opening.

As you become more relaxed with meeting energy in yourself, you find a natural extension of this happening with others. Pain energy in another is no different in any way from energy in your own system. It is all the same separated, totally impersonal energy seeking resolution, looking for Home. So you find yourself, if the situation is fitting, in direct, welcoming relationship with these balls of energy in another, bypassing the personality and issues and mechanisms of mind. A catalyst for the dissolution of pain in others, a totally organic movement of Love.

The Quan Yin of your heart is awakening. You come to see that You are Home, and all is invited and welcomed Here.

Exhausting the Personal Will

August 6

The ability to embrace pain and discomfort is not easily come by. Very often it is through the sheer mental exhaustion of resistance that the ripeness for welcoming appears.

This ritual of resisting/accepting happens many times over until gradually the futility of mind spinning is apparent, and the easing down into just Presence and sensation becomes a more natural way of being. Letting the emotional body release in whatever way it needs to is part of it all.

Even though the discomfort may well become more intense and acute as deeper aspects of ego surface, a whole new sense of space and purpose about what's really going on opens up. You are on board with the will of whatever is taking you Home.

Old habits of energy like collapsing into despair and hopelessness can no longer grab you. It's organic. You just can't go there anymore.

You are standing firm as the Truth, and you are grateful, grateful for all the discomfort, all the burning, all of the not-getting-what-you-want, because this is what is driving you back to the unwavering backbone of the Self.

To Want What's Here

August 10

To want what's here, even in disturbance, to recognize it as the gift of your very own Heart for you, to see it all as the totality of the Heart, nothing outside—this is grace. And this is peace.

This Love Affair of All Time

August 20

Is there anything more beautiful than the crushed, vulnerable ego being held by the Love it has surrendered into, has miraculously fallen into?

Over and over again, we fall into the Beloved's arms, this love affair of all time that takes us beyond time and into the Heavens where we cherish and are cherished for all eternity.

Dear Daughter, I Am Holding You Now

August 23

Some of us were mothers and fathers before we ever knew what it meant to be one, to honor a child's being, to care for their emotional needs. What did we know of that when we lived in ignorance of the beauty of our own being with our needs and wants exiled to that place where they were not even supposed to exist?

You can be a mother again. Those moments when you could not be there for your child, as presence, as love, as understanding, those moments are here now. If they are alive at all in your memory, in your being, they are here. Your four-year-old daughter is here, still crying out for understanding, still waiting for her mother.

You can hold her now. Let your heart open to her pain, to your pain of that time. It is one. A dynamic of energy appearing to be divided, in separate bodies. But there is no division, and this joint ball of pain energy waits patiently for the love of just one heart to dissolve it.

A moving, feeling kaleidoscope of love swelling, of tears, of asking forgiveness, of forgiving yourself, of union, of blessedness. And something comes to rest, something that was longing to come to the rest and calm and tenderness of the opened heart.

This is the beauty of how relationship serves us in our own Homecoming.

My Will or the Beloved's

August 27

My husband had brain cancer for many years. It went into remission due to some great alternative medicine, but his brain was damaged by that time, and he needed continuous caretaking.

I could not accept that the rest of my life was about caretaking. I fought it and fought it and cried and cried with despair for months… who knows how long… finally out of utter exhaustion I gave in, accepted that if this was what my life was about… OK. There was such peace afterwards.

There were still many, many moments of frustration and struggle but never to the same degree of wanting him to die so I could have "my" life back.

When the tears and fighting bottom out, it is grace to just get up in the morning and be in service to the Heart, whatever it looks like.

With gratitude for the classroom of life.

Let Yourself Be Humbled

August 31

Let yourself be humbled.

Let others have what you want.

Let your image and false sense of self be shredded.

Keep your head bowed down, close to the ground. It will rise of its own accord naturally, organically, majestically when all notions of a special somebody have been emptied out.

Committed Midwives

September 5

At a certain point, we notice a particular shift and it is a beautiful one. It is where we become committed to ourselves, committed to meeting all of ourselves, what is here now and what is still buried and hidden away.

It fuses with the growing recognition that what is here now is all that is true; it is the Beloved's offering, and it is the Beloved itself.

And we become committed midwives, staying open to all the contractions and visitations from the unconscious mind as it empties itself out. There is less tolerance for the useless, torturing thoughts around how "this" shouldn't be here or how there is something wrong with me because "this" is here… again.

It's a standing in Truth. A not-abandoning yourself any longer to thought or avoidance, and it becomes an all-out frontal engagement with what's here now.

We birth ourselves through the canals of conditioned consciousness and into the clear light of Heaven on Earth.

Kissing the Body

September 7

Do the aches and pains in your body really care about how many dry, hoping, "should-ing" thoughts you have about exercise or cutting this or that from your diet in the eternal search for wellness?

Here they are, calling out for the intimacy of your presence, for your mercy and holding, for the recognition that these too are, as all things, the face of Love.

Come on in home to your sweet body, here in every now, your friend, your life's companion… this blessed vessel of Love.

The Treasure Chest of the Body

September 10

Everything we have ever fled from, as separated consciousness, is here, right here in our body, in our nervous system. We don't have to travel far to know ourselves, to meet ourselves.

This fleeing the body is what keeps us bound. And now we have an even more sophisticated form of leaving ourselves—the use of spiritual concepts. How frequently the mind tries to chew on these, in one more valiant, exhausting effort to get away from the "ouch" of life, from what we are actually feeling, from the discomfort, the waves of angst that rise in the body.

Discomfort arising is a gift. It is the body's way of defrosting itself, of integrating the massive amount of old shock, separation energy that is stored there.

Don't deny your experience, even if you know at some level it's not real. Imagine telling an upset baby it doesn't exist. Where and how could that land? Let your experience become truly unreal by giving it the reality and attention it first needs. It is through this body of ours that we come to realize we are not the body.

Presence and sensation with no ownership of any of it: Our sanctuary, our favorite resting place, our true resting ground.

The Mystic's Cry

September 13

The crying out of all the mystics through the ages becomes our own song of yearning to the Beloved. The heart swells and breaks now with a different kind of purging—no longer associated with anything of this world but the yearning of a soul that can no longer go on without melting completely into her Beloved.

How close we stand now, so close to the Heart of God. What last steps would we not take to be this Love, to live this Love, to see the face of Christ, the face of the Beloved in all that stands before us and beside us and within us?

To stroke the Christ in the bodies of our brothers and sisters.

To see, to know their hearts, their light as our very own.

To die, to live again as gratitude for the sheer loveliness of pure Love.

Words to Myself

September 19

Find the Wellness in the midst of the fog of the mind. This Wellness that is light and bright and alive, that doesn't follow thought.

You are intent on clearing the fog, through any and all means that have been tried before, through thought itself, some substance, prayer, tears, supplication, reaching out to others.

It is the time, my love, to find Yourself. To find what needs no help. To stand your ground. Let the fog come and go, and go to come again.

What is always here, undisturbed, undefiled: This pilot light of Aliveness that never goes out.

A New Name

September 23

Dear Hearts,

I had a significant dream a month ago or so, and a new name came for me. It is "Pema." Pema is the Tibetan word for "lotus flower." It feels very fitting in that the lotus flower grows out of the mud and is untainted and unsoiled by it. Praise be.

I am very grateful to wear this name and to transition into it as it wants to happen.

With love,

Pema Mags

We Bow Down, We Bow Down, We Bow Down

September 25

What are you still rejecting, dear heart? What have you still not been able to love, even after all this time? Some addictive habit, some body ailment, some fear the character is "not supposed" to still have?

This very thing has Heaven written all over it, but all we ever see is the torment of it. This is the straw that breaks the camel's back, this that breaks the mind because it can no longer bear the weight of its resistance.

Dear brave characters that we have, Hafiz's "sweet crushed angels," burdened with the incredible weight of a life that is indisputably unresolvable. Can we honor their fortitude, their innocence and let them take rest?

Can we bow at last before Love appearing as "this"? Can we welcome the unfixable, knowing it is laden with the perfume of Heaven?

These brows of ours, so flat in form: were they made for anything other than their eventual placement on that grace-filled, holy Ground before the feet of God? Such light, such profound relief emanating from this Ground.

To take the ego by the hand, to lead it here, this is all that is wanted and hungered for. The end of separation, the end of suffering. The "re-entry" into the Heart of the Holy.

To Meet Everything as Love

September 29

These deep shamanic journeys that I have written about before were an offering of clarity and seeing into what is really going on underneath the layers of complicated, obscuring, everyday mind.

One of these journeys opened into great discomfort in the body and overall system. There was the usual reluctance to go towards it. Anything and everything was tried as a means of distracting from it. Making small movements, shifting physical position, looking around, thinking, the idea of going to the bathroom. Each time I would leave the discomfort and "go out," it would take a while to come back to the point where I had left off, but always returning to the exact same discomfort.

Lesson: distraction, resistance is futile.

At a certain point, there was an invitation, a distinct prodding and opening to see the discomfort as Love. There was an immediate sense of greater ease, of willingness to stay fully there, of lightening. Jesus and Devaji (my teacher) were present, holding my hands, and it was surprisingly peaceful. I felt great ability to meet anything with them beside me.

And then, I felt their hands slipping away and my own heart emerging in a stronger way and being told to go forward with just my own heart. It was fine. It was strong enough on its own to meet whatever came.

Later in that same journey, I experienced thoughts as strong voices taunting me:

You'll never make a living. You're useless. You know M. is going to go off with another woman and have a wonderful life. (Obviously my fears and beliefs showing up).

I could see them as not having any real substance at all—just taunting voices, and they passed away. The Heart was steady. It felt like Buddha sitting under the Bodhi tree. The overall repeating mantra was: *Stand as your own heart. Stand as the Heart. Stay in the Heart.*

May we stay here in the Heart.

Until You Emerge Softened

October 4

Let the hard edges of your being be eroded away.

Let others shine and receive the glory.

Your path is showered with the soft petals of humility until you emerge softened, yielding, and your relationship with the Heart and all that is has blossomed into a full-blown love affair.

The Belly of Pain

October 8

Walk into the belly of pain.

Let all your specialness be crumbled here, your sweet, innocent attempts to be a somebody, a somebody of note, a somebody at all.

You are walking into the cave of your Heart, a glorious nobody, this one shining Self.

A Blanket of Acceptance

October 13

Wrap yourself in a blanket of acceptance. Snuggle into the goodness, your own clear, light goodness. Bathe in the peace of nobody here and nothing mattering.

And let this be your baseline of existence, where you come to over and over again until it is known that this is Home and everything else is but a dream, unraveled and softened now by the light and ease of Love.

Come Outside the Dreamscape

October 20

Come outside the dreamscape. Come on outside and breathe the pure, fresh air of nothing happening, nothing needing your attention or fixing or loving.

Leave behind your nostalgia, your sentimentality, your fascination with this character of humanness and its unceasing struggle to make happiness and enlightenment its own.

Stand erect, like a pillar of light, unmoving, unswayed by the tugs of the dream. How sweet the sound of bells tinkling here, calling you to what is true and eternal.

Calling us Home to the loveliest vista of all: the land of the unbounded, passionate Heart.

As Love Embodies

October 26

Many of us experience much malaise in the body in this process of Love embodying itself. These dear bodies carry so much of the energetic weight of separation.

Initial resistance to the discomfort and burning is entirely normal, human. It is the function of the ego to resist. Be patient with these episodes of resistance, the mind spinning around what or who could help, the distraction and comfort seeking, the sheer "no" of it all.

At a certain point, we are graced to settle down and actually be present with what is here. Meeting sensation with thoughtless receptivity.

You become a large basin for the body's cries and aches. A going towards them organically happens in the recognition that they are your beloveds, your long-lost ones. You may even find yourself seeking their forgiveness for having cast them out for so very long, in lifetimes of unawareness and running.

And could there be anything sweeter in existence than this intimacy with all of Yourself, this reunion of Love with what was long lost to it?

Bearing the grace of the body's malaise, we come to know the delight, the connectedness, the intimacy of embodied Love.

From Disconnection to Intimacy

November 2

Our old, habitual ways of connecting with each other get stripped as we wade deeper into the waters of embodiment.

The coping mechanisms we had for covering up our shyness and introversion get painfully exposed. Gregariousness and conditioned speaking with a lot of energy begins to feel terribly false. The light is being shone on all the ways our inner sense of disconnection shows up, and we can be left standing awkward, self-conscious, one contracted lump of energy.

Simply allowing this energy of contraction to be here is all that is needed. It's no longer about trying to connect, but feeling and sometimes speaking the disconnection if that feels safe. We get to speak what could never be spoken, and there is profound relief in this alone.

And there may be such a longing in these moments to have someone hold you, to smooth out, to cry out the raw, defrosting threads of disconnection and separation in someone's understanding, compassionate arms. And this is pure grace. Love appearing through the dream, an extension, a reflection of your own softening heart.

The world, the life, is one big ache and cry of unlovedness and disconnection. But Love, as it moves in, connects with warmth and delight and great ease of being. The true embodied intimacy of the one Heart.

Being Triggered

November 12

Wherever the body-mind has been triggered, expect it to be triggered in that same arena many times over and over again, until you can stand undisturbed in the face of what was always a catalyst for pain.

Heralding in the end of all suffering.

And every triggering is orchestrated with the clear view, precision, and tailor-madeness of Love, in its deepest caring for you, in response to your original calling out for freedom.

O Blessed Vulnerability

November 16

Beloved, soft, soft place, how can it be that I never knew your name or where you lived before?

You that I love the most and have waited so long to see your face.

I could lay with you now forever.

You that lifts my arms to Love and has me call out Her name.

And Love comes running to meet me Here
For what could stand between us now
With all walls turned to dust in suffering's long embrace?

O most tender place of the human heart
How can I possibly write you or word you?
I simply bow in prayer
That all beings will, some day, call you dear.

Love as Shepherd

November 24

O, these places that don't know yet they are Love, that don't know how included they are in the All.

When one of these finally feels the touch of the Heart after eons in the dark, what a cascade of tears, of tenderness, of heart swelling, of gratitude, of utter commitment to know and be this Love everywhere.

The unraveling of what binds us to the dream of separateness as Love shepherds all back into the fold.

Self-Abandonment

November 27

Seeking love and attention outside yourself must be one of the ego's most well-trodden routes. Sparked by the unmet needs of the unloved one inside, our lives are a campaign of love-seeking. This "something unloved" will always be seeking attention, but it looks for it in wayward, off-the-mark ways, the only ways we've ever known.

But nothing from the outside can pierce through this shell of unintegrated energy. It can only break from within. It lies encased in itself until the pressure builds enough to break it open. And life conspires to build this pressure.

As it breaks, it hurts. And sometimes it hurts tremendously. But now we have enough wisdom to know there is no other way. Freedom is calling, and it will rupture what must be ruptured.

As energy-breaking-apart engulfs the system, it brings with it its own crystal-clear clarity: seeking anything outside yourself will only lead you back to pain. And layer by layer, Love's interventions dissolve the seeking one.

The self-abandonment eases up. The forays into the external look empty and dry. We come to rest more naturally, more gracefully in ourselves, in the moment, in whatever we are doing, being, right now. We enter and stay in the stream of our own life: a natural intimacy with ourselves, the lack of which spawned all the seeking.

The Imperfect One

December 6

Gradually, over time, we learn to hold space for even the most difficult of emotions and the gnarliest of issues. We watch as tenderness becomes an exquisite form of self-inquiry, dismantling the walls and armoring of the ego-construct in the most beautiful way.

And we realize, to our deep surprise and overwhelming gratitude, it was never about having the perfect life, personality, body, but that the sweet love that comes forth to hold the "imperfect" one is all that was ever wanted and hungered for. And this Love is our very own Self.

A Dream Road

December 12

This moment is the final destination. It is the end of the journey, the all-across-the-road cul-de-sac sign. Just This.

If you must, turn around and take a last look back at that long road you've been traveling forever on. The sheer length of it, the arduousness of it, the hills, the valleys, the detours, the bypasses, the maze of it all, the pain of it all.

A dream road that was only, always a declaration of your wrongness, your unlovedness. A wrong "somebody" that has never existed, that was never separate from the shining reality of Truth.

Meet yourself here in this moment. Meet every teacher you've ever had Here. Everyone you have ever loved, friend, child, lover, animal. They are all Here, whether it is known or not.

What do we do Here? We do nothing. A big, giant nothing. Hanging out in nothingness. Vaguely felt, thin, flat, it doesn't matter. We stay Here.

And the more you give yourself to this, the more it gives itself to you. And this nothing gradually reveals itself to have depth, great depth, the depth of existence itself. Nothing outside it, everything happening within it, and it is You.

A Great, Full-Bodied Now containing everything, in which all things appear.

Love's Priceless Offering

December 14

Take care when you notice the thought arising about how tired you are of some patterning or life situation or how you can't wait to be free of it. This situation is Love's priceless offering to you, a classroom that is individualized for you beyond perfection. Relax into the grace of it and remember this is what is taking you Home.

Receiving Energy, Receiving the Ego

December 18

Everything that feels separate in the system must come into the openness. And it's the job of our life circumstances to trigger and activate just this.

As old energy rises to the surface, it flounders around initially. It presents itself as confusion, small child, not-on-firm-ground feelings, very busy mind darting around reciting all that's wrong with you. It activates the "groove" of the particular aspect of suffering that your body-mind carries. What has always been wrong with you is still what's wrong. Wherever you have gone historically, this is where you go again. It can look like depression, anxiety, hopelessness. No new issues. No new feelings.

It is just energy. We cannot say this often enough: it is just energy. Energy being siphoned off and returning Home. If there were no interpretation of it, it would be a breeze.

So, it's to let this energy do what it needs to do. There is nothing comfortable about it. So be it for a while.

Find what nurtures you in these moments. Cry it out some; storm it out if necessary. If it has settled into a knot in the body, sit with it or hold space for it. Energy does not necessarily move through in the blink of an eye. It takes time, patience, holding. Just like a baby.

Of course, what the energy is looking for most of all is Love. Ordinarily we know this but find we cannot turn Love on with the flick of a switch. "May Love come to this" is a sweet mantra that can help tease open the heart. Even in the reciting of it there is already great awareness of the bigger picture of what is going on. We can call on the strength and love of

Ramana, Jesus, Ammachi, any form of Love that resonates with our heart. This can help greatly.

The heart may open or not. If not now in these moments, it surely will later in its own sweet time.

The flurry of energy passes, mind becomes substantially quieter. Gratitude moves in, organic gratitude, natural to every single heart. Life looks bright and open again; Love has emptied us out one more time.

The Sweet Ease of a Loved Being

December 23

What a strange paradox that much of our awakening work lies in coming to tender peace with what we seek to wake up from—the imagined "me." Most of our lives are spent convinced that happiness lies in fixing up the personality and the body. We toil away at our self-improvement habits and hopes, trying to find a foothold on okayness.

But the ego will never be OK in its own eyes. It is far from natural to us to be gentle with ourselves. There isn't a cell in our bodies that is DNAed to love our own beings.

This world of bodies and form was birthed with and from the belief that we are separate from Love. As programmed egos, we are walking, moving automatons of unlovedness.

How does the great tide of the Heart turn finally towards this innocent creature-being?

The great discomfort, the constant offness, the pain of self-rejection must make itself known. That foothold of okayness becomes a very slippery ground that can no longer provide the false security it once did. Love is only intent on exposing what is unloved. This exposure is a nightmare for the ego. All that's wrong with you, everything you cannot fix is swimming before your love-starved eyes. Whether it is body issues or personality issues, something looks unresolvable. Love has you smack in its embrace, cornered, stuck, unredeemable.

We must bear the discomfort of this place. This spot is the very gateway into the Heart. No other entrance point is available. And it opens, it always opens, doing its own work, the mysterious alchemical work of the Heart.

And everything softens again. The convincing issue collapses. Love for the self peers through, and you would not want yourself, your life to be any different than the pure perfection of the moment. The sweet ease of a loved being.

And this is all you have to love. In loving this being, we love the whole world of the being. The end of projection, the end of denial. The preparation for the full dismantling of a separate individual.

Speaking Our Truth

December 28

Good behavior won't take you home. It served us as well as it could but breaking out of the box of conditioning is a whole new playing field.

Some of us have great difficulty in speaking our truth. We qualify and justify and explain. We preamble what we really want to say, trying to be inoffensive, trying to soften things for other minds. We hold back, hide, squash down our truth. It may be the expression of a need (when the conditioning has been that it's not OK to have needs). It may be the honest, open relating of some true feelings, of vulnerability, of hurt, sadness, anger.

Spiritual knowledge can compound the issue because now we want to be loving and spiritual, and we know that much of our relative truth is coming from mistaken identity, so we hold back even more, trying to be loyal to the absolute truth that there is only Love, only silence, only peace.

But the great beauty is that our relative truth, when expressed as the truth of what's here in the moment, is the Absolute. No distinction. Just Truth. The fine mist at the top of the fountain is as much the truth as the great surge at the base, as much the truth as the stillness that fuels the surge.

Stop holding back this natural flow of energy. Stop deadening yourself. Come alive into this one, organic flow.

It's about firing the editor. It's about expressing ourselves, truly, openly, honestly, not deflecting with mind monitoring and caretaking.

As Truth starts prying open the box of conditioning, there may be a lot of fear and confusion as to what expressing our truth really means. What if we hurt someone? What if we lose something precious? This is all to be expected, and patience and gentleness with our fear is all part of it.

There is no tried-and-true formula for how to be. It's an adventure for each of us. No one can introduce us to this free land—only ourselves as our courage and discernment grow around the fine lines of being loving, being true, being open.

Out of the box. Speaking what could never be spoken. Free-flowing. Oh, the joy and expansion of it. Always landing on greater energy, refreshing truth, a heart free now to love truly.

Orna, Pema's older daughter, with her mom

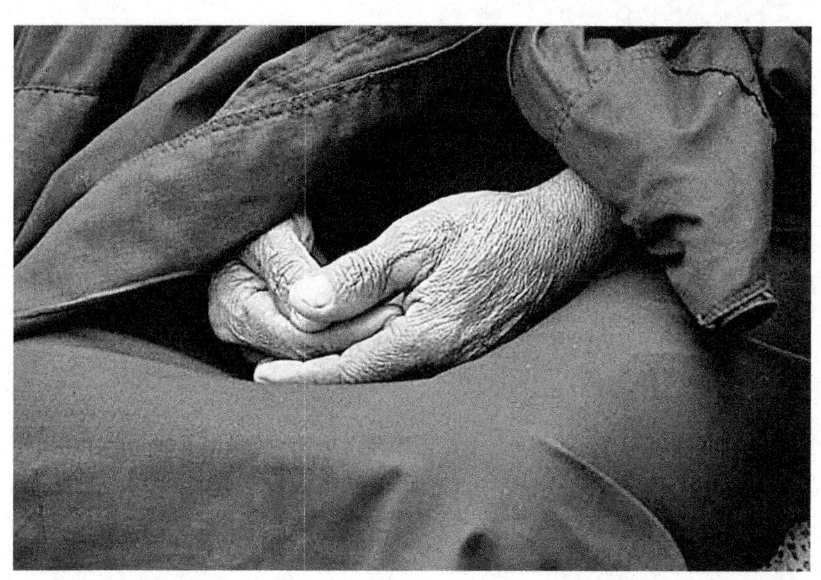

2012

Goodwill

January 5

How beautiful it feels to let others have what you want. To see the specialness, the attention you have craved go to another and to have reached that place in your heart where rejoicing is the outcome. This is one of the places where our inner work inevitably leads.

The humbling of the ego, the erosion of personality posturing ushers in a new kind of glory. It's a quiet, inner resurrection of completeness in Yourself that naturally extends out in goodwill, in love and support for others.

Move Freely

January 10

If you hold back from following your heart, from simply doing what you want to do in the moment for fear of offending others, for fear of what they might think, this is the ultimate deadener. It is the sadness of life given that cannot be lived.

Act as if you're alone even when others are present. Move freely.

Speak the truth, be the truth, do the damn thing you want to do.

We Rise Up

January 14

We rise up in the midst of darkness. We do not wait, bound to the dark, until it miraculously fades away.

Rise up, dear heart, rise up. Let the mind fall away from this pillar of Truth that You are.

It is time to stop believing the chaos, to take that Stand that ignores thought.

Do we really need any more evidence, any more time to realize the mind is a battle field? One thought pitting itself against the next, a ricochet of taunts and barbs, a world at war with itself and only itself. A revolving door of pain and pleasure.

Leave the battlefield. Don't wait for enough healing, enough self-love, enough redemption.

And savor the delight of true Stance, where you are unaffected, undisturbed by all appearance.

To Call Myself Beloved

January 18

Compassion for ourselves is not easily wrung out of us. The price, so often, is some unacceptable part of our lives intensifying in its very unacceptability.

That mind has already exhausted itself in the search for resolution is a great blessing. Nothing to do now but wait. Waiting for that surprising moment when the heart bursts open, sometimes stimulated by an act of kindness, a touch of grace from the external.

New levels of tenderness for ourselves, for all of life, are forged open, and we rest again in the dear, dear sweetness of the Heart.

And did you get what you wanted from this life, even so?

I did.

And what did you want?

To call myself beloved, to feel myself beloved on the earth.

~ Raymond Carver

The Offering of Stuckness

January 23

When stuckness in some area of life prevails, it is the highest offering of all. It is what keeps inviting you to step fully outside the mind.

Body ailments, financial distress, unrealized desires, addictions… whatever it may be, be assured it is serving you greatly. Left to our own devices in the mind, all things going relatively well, what enticement is there to leave it? Continuing to identify with it must become extremely disagreeable or no serious stepping back, stepping out of it, will materialize.

Stuckness is usually where you've circled for years, mapping out a small parcel of mind where, despite the suffering, you get to hold on to the familiarity of something you must resolve, a great problem, something that unconsciously binds you and holds you in separation.

It is where the Beloved is kissing you most fervently with a "Come, dear heart, come Home to Me." Its supreme gift to you is the beginning of the end of you.

It may not feel in your best interest, but you must leave the exhausting merry-go-round of fixing, of seeking resolution, of betterment. You are not abandoning anything except the unreal.

Let yourself be airlifted out of stuckness, out of mind. You are not the mess, not the body, not the face you see in the mirror every morning and are so convinced is you.

You are a fountain of clarity inside that is still and yet bubbles with goodness and delight and joy. Let us come Home. And let us stay Home.

There is Nobody Out There

January 29

Some years back I was graced with the stark seeing that there is nobody out there. This appeared in the midst of a deep shamanic journey. I was imagining reporting something to a friend and then, suddenly, with an "Oh my God," she disappeared and it was seen clearly that she didn't exist. The mind's perception of her just did not exist.

It was hard to look at; the mind wanted to curl back into itself and not look at the truth: that it is speaking to itself and only itself all the time. That every thought, judgment, feeling we have that seems to be about another originates in us, and is only about US.

Although engraved somewhat in my system, this seeing faded, and it is only now, after years of meeting projections onto others, that this truth is being rekindled.

If it serves you, remind yourself regularly that there is nobody out there. Notice how there is a pulling back in from the external, a natural self-containment that happens, an opening back into the formlessness of your true nature.

Opening back into Absolute Reality, this formless, perceptionless seat of peace, stillness, radiance.

Let Yourself Be Deeply Touched

February 7

Let yourself be deeply touched when goodness shines on the places that have not known it before.

Love comes to you in an unexpected way, perhaps from an unexpected source, and as it comes to you, something rushes to meet it from inside. It is energy that has been cordoned off, shut down in your system, and it pours forth now in tears and gratitude and a recognition of what has been missing.

Let this have its full life, let all the energy of it be released. Healing is happening in the sweetest, most pain-free way there is, leaving your heart more open to receive and give the goodness of Love.

The Holding

March 5

Let what is full hold what feels lacking. Let what needs no attention hold what longs for it.

Over and over again, we hold the lost parts and energies as they emerge slowly and gradually out of the unconscious dark, until their innocence and lovedness is known through and through, and the holding itself becomes our savored experience.

The Force of Pain

March 12

Let every ache of mistaken identity surface and be felt until the force of pain itself would burn away this false collusion with an illusionary character.

And finally, you come to see that pain has done its work, and true seeing fills the space where once such pain arose.

And now you stand again where you have always stood, free of trappings and imaginings, free to be and free to see. And all are known to be as close to you, as one with you, as the very one you thought you were.

Cleaning Up Our Act

March 16

I remember years back reading about the spiritual sage, Byron Katie's journey and how at one point, she started feeling the presence of this voluptuous old lady in a paisley dress with a bun in her hair. This lady felt like pure love to her and whenever Katie was out of integrity as in telling a lie, exaggerating a story for effect, the lady would recede and Katie could no longer feel the love. Desperate to have her back, Katie would do whatever had to be done to make amends, calling people to apologize and to tell the truth. And she would again feel the love of her lady and all would be well.

I remember longing to have a little old lady or some such loving figure show up in my awareness and help me clean up my act.

But the truth is that Love has not forgotten any of us, and we have a built-in mechanism for knowing when we are out of integrity. As mature seekers, we begin to become acutely aware of when we're off. We know when we're being dishonest in subtle ways, we know when we're doing a little self-promotion, we know when we're holding back information that might make someone else look good. Oh, we know a lot of things. And if we don't, and our commitment to truth is in place, the feedback or reflection of our off-ness from the external will appear in no short measure.

So, the invitation is to clean up our act. Be honest and direct. Tell the truth. Make those calls when necessary, and say you're sorry. And don't hold back on helping others to shine when it feels appropriate.

And when we can't, can we have the utmost patience and understanding for the one who feels fearful? In God's timing, we all come to see we could never lose anything of value by being true. We only gain our whole life back.

The Energy of Aversion

March 27

All the distaste, aversion, dislike I feel towards another is towards my own self. The distaste is in me, with me, only me.

The other is not really there, just a convenient object in consciousness to project the ego's self-hatred onto because it is unbearable to feel the brunt of that in its entirety.

It has been unconscious, but through the gift of this other, it is no longer hidden and buried.

Once we get over the initial blaming and story, we sit with the sensations of aversion, remembering it is never about the other, recognizing this energy of aversion is ripe and ready and wanting to come home. And gratefully, this is what is happening in the holding of it… it is coming home.

The End of Personal Will

April 9

At certain moments you realize you want only what God wants for you. Any other kind of wanting or self-serving becomes too painful to bear.

These moments repeat themselves. We don't just surrender an issue, and that's the end of it. The little, separate self reasserts itself many times over; we surrender many times over. Each time the weight and drive of the personal will is eased until eventually there is only the One Will.

Ancestral Energies

"The personal self is no more than the point person of all your ancestral energies."

~ Adyashanti

April 16

Your mother, your father, your grandparents all live in your body. What lay buried in their bodies for lifetimes was taken in by yours through some form of energetic osmosis.

How incredibly personal it all feels. How incredibly impersonal it truly is. Just shrouds of energy traveling down through the halls of time.

Can we open to what surfaces in our system, recognizing its long history, its long search to be free?

Bring your ancestors home. Give the mind back to God where it belongs. Let it all come to its final resting place.

The Divine Archer

May 5

Triggers are a vital part of the freeing process. They push up against what is repressed, pulling and plucking energy out of seclusion and confinement. They gradually and systematically thin out the force of conditioning and the magnetic pull into the small self, until the web of ego is diffused enough to be actually seen as illusion.

Triggered energy coming loose can feel jumbled and chaotic. Sometimes you don't even know what the precise hurt is; you just know you feel awful.

Writing down or stating the things that upset you can be helpful in the process of digestion and integration, being specific and totally childish. If you can, when you can, write them in the form of a thank you.

There is just something about saying "thank you" for what is challenging that helps open the energy of it, release the tears of hurt, and at the same time, a higher seeing is happening around how exactly this is serving you.

It can lift you out of victim mentality and into the recognition that it is only the small "me" that is being deconstructed with the mind-blowing precision of the divine archer.

And You, oh blessed You, are as intact and as invulnerable as before, during and after any dream of individuality came into appearance.

Jealousy—One Road Home

June 5

Certain individuals feel the brunt of jealousy to a great degree. Others rarely experience it. As it is not the most wholesome state of mind to admit to, especially in spiritual circles, let us be assured that those who experience it as a recurring theme are holding a one-way ticket home in their shaky, insecure hands.

Jealousy springs from core beliefs of unworthiness, lack, feeling not-good-enough. Particular constructs are hard-wired to externalize this lack and live in a story of "they have it, and I don't." In earlier years, our desires being the typical ones of the collective, we envy those who have success, money, beauty, love relationships. At this stage it is somewhat manageable as the shell of the ego is quite intact, and we don't necessarily feel that much.

As we mature spiritually, our desires shift to awakening or special attention from a spiritual teacher or something in the world that still binds us. We have now entered the crucible of truth, and there is no returning. The jealousy of those who apparently have what we want is acute and painful. The shell of the ego is well punctured now, and we feel everything more intensely. At moments you feel like you are the pettiest thing on the planet, but you are so far from that. You are doing the most challenging work of a lifetime, meeting a replay, a symptom of the original pain of separation from God, coming up against the place where the construct was first formed.

There is no avoiding this pain. It does its holy work, not only interrupting beliefs of lack but dismantling the very one who believes anything at all. It is seen that there is nobody out there, the world of "have" and "have-nots" recedes from our interest, and the so-envied spiritual prowess, as interpreted by the mind, is known to be lifeless cardboard.

The aliveness and freshness of our true nature is being tasted, and the gratitude we feel for the characters in our dream who helped point us back here is sweet beyond measure.

Holding Our Human Frailty

June 11

Take yourself on your lap. The image of yourself, just as you are today. Maybe your hair is long since grey, your limbs feel old and stiff, nothing is as quick and smart as it once was. The promise and hope of fixing, of making better, the endless attempts to be once again in a vibrant body, all have been eroded and exhausted into nothing to do but be here now. All avenues are closed except the one of Love.

Hold this broken one. Stroke the limbs that have given all they've got, these limbs of God that you have called your own. This dear body and being that you have harshed and prodded and twisted into so many moves that were never their truth.

Let her rest now. Let this "sweet, crushed angel" rest in the tenderness that her very vulnerability draws forth in such equal measure. Your holding arms become the arms of the Great Mother, your lap is God's lap, your heart is infused with that love that folds everything into itself.

Tears of vulnerability give way to those of gratitude for right seeing, for the miracle of what you really are. These bodies are on their way out, but this Love is our eternal nature, the Promise that lies beneath all worldly promises that "come and go and go to come again."

Anger and Hatred

"The holiest of all the spots on earth is where an ancient hatred has become a present love."

~ A Course in Miracles

June 18

Honor your anger and hatred. Let it arise in the body and run its natural course. There is a time and place for all things. Yes, it is all only about you, but we must see it to clear it. It cannot be freed unless it arises.

Wallow in the mental thinking as little as possible, and sit with the bare bones of the sensation of it in your body. Be fully available for it.

On the heels of hatred is this surprising warmth and love. The love that was always there through the drama. And gratitude for the one who showed you the extent of your own self-denigration and helped you free it.

There Is Nothing for You in This World

June 26

There is nothing for you in this world. To truly take this in is huge, and we do it at the pace ordained for us.

We must turn our backs on it all. Turning away from the thrill of specialness, approval, attention. Have no concern about how to do this. It gets done for us. It is taken from us… by Love, which is simultaneously offering in its other hand the beauty and light of our true nature.

Being a Non-Believer of Mind

July 2

Joy arises at times in the simple sitting with whatever is here in the moment, the knowing that this is as close as we can come to God right now.

So we sit with what's here. The myriad changing sensations, the errant thought that makes your tummy curdle, the energy of propulsion that really, really wants to move and do the next thing.

But we sit tight, unmoving, being a non-believer of mind. We sit like the Buddha sat. Each and every one of us is the Buddha, and we are all called in our own time to take a stand for what is real. Meeting illusion in the exact same way as all the sages have.

The dream was never supposed to be good—the ego's miscreated world, a gigantic mass of energy twirling around on itself, endlessly changing form, going absolutely nowhere. Seeking, seeking, never finding the Ground. For how can anything other than separation be found within a bubble of separation?

Watch. Witness. Notice what you notice. Do not believe it.

What A Good Ego Does

July 28

The ego taunts. It taunts you. This is a symptom of its own self-hatred, arising from the collective unconscious guilt and pain from the original separation.

There is nothing unique or personal or special about self-denigrating thoughts. It's just what a good ego does. Every mind does this until the lie of it is known.

We must get used to not having what we want, to the character not having the gifts and qualities we would like it to have. There is a great feeling of strength and relief when we can recognize that the character is just a byproduct of the conditioning field we were born into. When we don't expect it to be more than that, there is peace.

See it from the Truth. Get that distance going between You and the programmed character, as if there are two of you. Viewed from Here, a natural gentleness and understanding comes for the limitations of the construct, the limitations of the family, the ancestry, the culture you inhabited.

And this limitation: how we are so not that.

Right Movement

August 4

Fatigue, nervous exhaustion, any compromise of the body is a pure blessing in lining us up with the true movement of our heart. It gradually knocks out all the deeply patterned tendencies to seek love and approval through pleasing and self-sacrifice.

When we extend ourselves in a way that is not true, the byproduct is even more exhaustion.

We cannot really digest sophisticated teachings like "no preference" until we have learned to stand our ground in the simple but revolutionary act of putting ourselves first.

Divinity meets humanity when the strength comes to step out of the patterned box and declare what our need is in each moment. And when the strength is not yet here, we lovingly hold that dear child-ego that still believes her source of love is out there in the external world. Or we simply notice what is happening. All preparation for the transformative action that will inevitably blossom.

There is such a force of well-being and aliveness that erupts when the tug of conditioning is no longer in charge. It is the roar of a heart held down way too long by the manipulative but innocent tethers of pleasing and sacrifice.

Intimacy

August 20

Intimacy with another, speaking what is here all the way through, not holding back any of those little scraps you fear would leave you exposed and open to the winds of littleness and un-togetherness.

Speak your heart, dear one, and watch yourself dissolving in a sweet pool of relief, softness and humility.

So simple and yet at times, it calls on every ounce of spiritual courage we've got.

Specialness

"Specialness is the ego's version of love."

~ *A Course in Miracles*

August 23

The ego absolutely craves specialness. In my experience, life takes care of the letting go of specialness and any clinging to personal attributes or possessions or relationships that seem to sustain it.

We are brought through a period where the places we hold on to for specialness are kind of taken from us. It will either seem to look like that, or it will literally happen. Either way there's a burning up of the beliefs that we are an important somebody.

So, there's burning… and there's also the watching of where "specialness thoughts" arise. And we can be gentle with those thoughts, just seeing them as typical ego, nothing to condemn at all. If we recoil from them, we give them more life.

We Are the Maker of It All

September 3

"Something wrong with me" / "unworthy" / "not good enough" is a compacted, dense energy form and belief that literally CREATES its own world, its own dream, its own bubble of form in which every molecule of energy is moved and sourced by "something wrong with me."

The content of mind is what causes the movement of the figures that people our world. We look out and what do we see? Only scenes and interactions and situations that we immediately INTERPRET to mean "something wrong with me."

What we don't realize, because it is obscured from us by the complexity of mind, is that we projected out the whole thing in the first place. Our external reality is a pictorial representation of our insides.

We are not the hapless victim of any of it. At a level of mind not conscious to us now, we are the maker of it all.

The knowing of this is very empowering and relieving.

The Unresolvable Issue

September 10

The unresolvable issue is truly the Holy's fierce and loving offering. Exhaustion with it actually starts to feel good. Nowhere else to turn now but to the Beloved.

And there is great peace in the realization that not being able to fix something is not a problem at all. We're not supposed to be able to fix it. It's the ego dying, and this is so much greater, so much more glorious, than any "perfect" dream that has no meaning at all.

Can we relax into the unfixable; could we even celebrate it?

Bodily Phenomena Emerging

September 20

Old, old, ancient energies seeping through our systems now. All manner of bodily phenomena emerging, releasing itself. Who are we to argue with one ounce of God's holy work?

Let us weep and shake and sound and hold space for all of it. A precious, tender, receiving Womb for the long held-in pain of believing we are here at all.

We are so big and unshakable now, so practiced in the divine art of meeting ourselves. For we know now that what looks and feels like darkness are just these lost, suffering, innocent clouds looking for Heaven.

And Heaven we are. And Heaven's gates we open to those clouds in the simple receiving of what is here now.

And how willingly they come now, these exhausted, broken

ones; how dear and tender and complete is the love that rises to greet them. A divine fusion and homecoming. Heart waters break and flow profusely. Body and eyes soften and glisten. And peace abides.

Rising Out of Misidentification

October 5

Many of us in this extremely challenging and beautiful time of Self-realization go through periods where the experience of having a vital and energetic body is a distant memory. And every attempt to restore wellness eventually comes back to ground zero. We are left with "nothing works" and "no control." Grounded by Love.

This is the time to let all ruminations about fixing go and simply receive the offering of the aches and pains of a broken body. This is the time to see that every ache is like a kiss from the Beloved saying, "Not here, love. Not here." The answer is not here in the body. Not only is the answer not in fixing it; it is nowhere near the body at all.

It is found in the seeing that a well body and a broken body are one in kind; they are both illusion. That a clear, light body has no more value than a body filled with energy that is purging and releasing—they are both imagined into existence.

It is cultivated in the gentle, firm and knowing "so what" and "nothing matters" arising in the face of unwellness.

The body's welfare is pre-ordained, the script already written. Can we walk through the play holding its hand, letting the newly-shining truth of its unreality and "not mattering" open the heart to great mercy and tenderness for all that is not real? Mercy for the unresolvable issue in our lives, whatever that may be, for how in its unwavering relentlessness, it is waking us up out of the heart of misidentification; its tugs on our attention, losing strength through the sheer exhaustion of its known ineffectuality.

We rise up as true Self in the midst of the unfixable. This is its job, and this is its grace. The rising up of the internal Real that sheds light on the unreality of all that is temporal.

The Most Important Question

October 16

Let yourself breathe, live, love, drown in the question, "Who?"

Who doesn't feel well? Who doesn't know what to do? Who needs to come out of the box? Who needs attention? Who is tired and achy? Who did a good job? Who is having a wave of angst? Who is crying? Who feels loving?

For every thought, feeling, action, there's a "who" waiting to take the wind out of its ownership sails.

Let all your resolve now be on the heart of the matter: a full-blown shift in identification from the character to the Self. Don't dilly-dally any longer in trying to make the character whole and shining and smelling good. Or fix up the character's lot in any way. It is futile. A shiny character cannot come Home any more than its not-so-shiny neighbor. Home and identified character can never meet. There is no point of intersection.

The belief in a "you" is the awful joke. There is no Santa Claus; there is no you. There was no Big Bang and everything we see, hear, smell, feel, think has been imagined into existence. When we know this to be true, all the way through, the suffering will end.

Marry your attention to the heart and hold on tight with all your might to your Beloved. He has been waiting throughout time for you and rejoices without measure in your Homecoming.

A Special Secret

November 9

There comes a point for those of us on the journey of the heart where adversity begins to be felt as a special secret between you and your Beloved. The challenges are recognized to be the precise and grace-filled offerings you need to open to the totality of the heart, to open to the precious vulnerability and fragility that is taking you beyond it to the invulnerability of your own Self.

Such a complete package of tears and beauty and love and strength and knowing and truth.

The sense of being victimized falls away; the need to speak of the difficulty of it all falls away because here you are in a cocoon of love and trust with your Beloved.

You are indeed the special one, the chosen one, not in the way your dear construct longed for or could ever have envisaged, but here it is, where every ache of body and mind generates the feeling of the Heart wrapping its shawl of Love around all of you in the most personal, close and complete way. You are Home, and all is indeed very, very well.

The Prodigal One

November 21

Hold this bundle of ineptitude you call "you." She that doesn't exist… but yet before she disappears into the mists of time, let us love her first so completely and tenderly and gratefully that no part of her need ever rise again to look for something in the eyes and heart of what could not bless her or see her innocence.

We stroke this being of body and mind with all of its ingrained habits of energy that we have struggled and sought so valiantly to fix and better. All in vain. She could never be more than she was. Not one step of hers was ever out of line, every movement the perfect product of a decision made long ago to be out on her own and make a body her home.

But this body is not her home, and neither were the countless ones she thought were hers before. Decisions made that seemed so real leading to worlds of form that now seem so real.

But Home we did not leave nor ever could. The loveliness of God is always ours, awaiting only our soul's holy and courageous choice to lay aside our toys and idle dreams, to make our home anew and rest again where we and God would have us be.

"Let Thy Will Be My Pleasure"

December 3

Thank you, Beloved, for bones that creak and limbs that ache, for age and fragility and dysfunction.

For systems that no longer work so well, for nothing being as smart and quick as it once was. For a mind dulled and fogged and wondering how it can go on.

For repeating thoughts of missing minerals and exercise not done. Seeking either to self-condemn or foolishly believe I can better or control.

For showing me the magnitude of identification with this bag of bones I call my body, I think is me.

All of this I need to come to You. You loosen these hands that claw and grasp at body wellness as if it were my ticket Home. Prying my fingers and gaze off yet another worldly prize and opening to what does not even know of such a world.

I bow down, Beloved, to You, to You that knows so refiningly well what this dear soul needs.

The Indian sage, Ramana Maharshi said, "Let Thy will be my pleasure." And may it always be.

Specialness Gives Way to Love

December 17

The ego needs specialness like the body needs water. The crumbling of the small self necessitates an entering into the areas where it has gotten its specialness in life or where it craves it.

These areas were perhaps unconscious to you, but they become glaringly more conscious as separated energies come closer to the Heart.

Loss of specialness for the ego is no walk in the park. It can be experienced as a slow burn over time or as intense periods of feeling like you're being raked over the coals. By the time we reach these core spots of ego, we are well-versed in the ways of the heart and the pain is often laced with beauty and tenderness.

Love seems to be woven into and through the fabric of the energies that are being loosened and reclaimed. The Gift-Giver is never far away from his Gift, and our tears now are a divine duet of hurt and blessedness.

Specialness gives way to Love, and layer by precious layer, the joy and vibrancy of the Heart is re-known.

All Things "Prodigal" Come Home

December 29

Let us take our grasping, fixing hands off the screen of the dream. Just to lift them off.

To recognize there is nobody out there. And neither is my body.

Whatever seems to be causing the distress is not really there.

The distress is all already inside me. The discomfort I am aware of was projected out onto images, scenes, people, my body… making it look like these are causing the discomfort. It is all the other way around. The original pain in the system is the author, the projector of the dream.

So, we come back to the disturbance; we withdraw all attention from the external, and our job is to bear the disturbance.

This is a mighty recognition and can cut through an enormous amount of torment and mind spinning.

So here we are with disturbance. All that's asked of us is to receive it. To receive what is already here, what is already in the process of self-liberating. A layer of energy has surfaced from the unconscious and its very presence shows its willingness to be dissolved.

Love rushes to meet her long lost children. This may not be our experience yet, but can we greet them? Can we say "hello?" Can we be glad that what is driving our dream of suffering is arising and returning to peace?

All things "prodigal" come Home. All things eventually weary of hardness and unkindness. All things deep inside secretly long for love. Sons of ego come to flicker in the shadows a while but eternally, truly, always Sons of God.

"For this son of mine was dead and is alive again; he was lost and is found." Luke 15:11-32

2013–2015

Skewered by Love

January 13

I have written several times before about a series of shamanic journeys I undertook in the Peruvian jungle some years back. Beautiful and sometimes shocking truths about the nature of Reality and illusion were seen and imbibed. Because these openings were shamanically induced and not a natural, organic evolution of my being, they faded, but the memory of what was glimpsed is often, often revisited and serves to open the heart in many challenging moments.

On one of these journeys, the experience opened into incredible pain. It felt like something was coming for me and I was going to be skewered, annihilated. Like the center would be taken out of me. "Centrified" was the word that came, and it felt unbearable (It was only later that I realized the feeling was of terror. I had never consciously experienced terror, and so the ability to label it was missing).

The intensity eased up, and then I circled around in mind, for a long time in great fear of "it" returning to get me. Circling, avoiding, it felt like I could live lifetimes of ordinary suffering rather than go back to face what was there at the core.

At some point out of sheer exhaustion, I turned to Mother and asked her to take me back.

The experience opened into this invitation to give up what was important to me in life. My daughters, the pleasure of sweet conversations with people. Then came my ex, to whom I was still emotionally attached. Giving up the sweetness of the romantic, special love relationship. I was finally able to do that.

And out of nowhere came the question, *Was I willing to give up thought?*

I circled with that for a long time. There was so much fear to be without thought, nothing to locate "me," to anchor "me," the personal construct. Not to be able to describe what was happening ever again, to be swallowed up in the nothingness.

Utterly exhausted with mind spinning, I was finally able to surrender to this.

And then arose the most beautiful experience of coming home to my dear Father, like the return of the prodigal son. Such incredible release from all the suffering. Being embraced in the most loving arms. My heart broke open, and the tears of gratitude, of overwhelming gratitude, flowed for a long time. My Father was so happy to have me home. Jesus, my teacher, was there, and it was a full rejoicing.

My only job now was to love. Nothing else. Just to love, to love, to love. To live the very simple way of love, nothing complicated. There was such purity in this love, a thrilling purity. A deeply personal love where everything about me is adored. All of the humanness and little personal ways of being that sometimes brought shame, all so incredibly sweet in this great love.

There was an outpouring of love for all the people in my life and an overwhelming, oh-so-beautiful gratitude for everyone I ever had difficulty and conflict with. The recognition that these people had brought me to this love.

Over and over again, I was reassured that my experience of love and loving is very simple, just like this felt. Just the heart pouring open in tears, in hugs. Not necessarily blissed out states of love as I sometimes imagined it should be.

I kept returning to my Father to be reassured he would be there loving me as all the specialness and impurities were cleaned away as the work of my life continued.

And so, it does continue, continues for all of us until it is known that the Heart is everything, the Heart is all, the Heart is all there is.

Everything is Coming Out of You

December 27

Everything is coming out of you. Your mind is a projector, projecting out all the circumstances of your life, all the characters you see, the appearance and sensations of your body, the feeling of being a person.

It's not your brain or your conscious mind that is projecting. Consciously you would never choose half of what you experience or all of it at times, indeed.

It is all arising out of your unconscious mind, what you are unaware of. Arising from one big, fat belief in separation and fragmentation and the ensuing pain and self-hatred that goes with this belief. The will, the willfulness of ego.

The beauty of this projected dream is that it is your road Home. Every tiny scrap of it that upsets you or triggers you is pointing you, pushing you back to what is Real.

Where the ego sees pain and real figures and a concrete world, God sees nothing. Because it is all a wisp of a dream, a hallucination of mind.

And so, we turn to our Holy Self in every disturbance and ask to know the truth. What is the truth here, Beloved? Please help me to see with Your Holy Eyes.

Belief in the reality of ego is what binds it, taking it seriously, forgetting to smile gently on the folly of it all.

We learn to look lightly at what the ego has made. Holding the hand of one who sees truly—Jesus, Ramana, the Holy Spirit, our Father—we look with and through their eyes of only Love. Illusion evaporates. And joy and great gratitude arise as we come to see yet once again, how incredibly invulnerable, untouchable, immortal we are in truth.

2016

Surrender

January 7

Surrender everything. Every single thought of lack and limitation and "don't know what to do."

Empty the mind of all that is keeping you hostage. Hand it back to the One you took it from—wanting to be more than the One, to be your own person, your own, independent, special agent.

Perhaps there is an ocean of tears as you bow down gratefully to the One who knows.

And what remains. What You are: peace and quiet and space and ease and the surety that all is very, very well indeed.

"Give Him your thoughts, and He will give them back as miracles which joyously proclaim the wholeness and the happiness God wills his Son, as proof of his eternal Love."

- A Course in Miracles

A God Walk

January 18

Walking in the sunshine and freshly-fallen snow, the whiteness and purity all around seems to reflect my eternal and longed-for innocence.

Tears and thank yous flow to God, to all the characters in my dream, their dearness, their beingness, their hearts. That exquisite blending of divinity with humanity, where Love rushes to meet our vulnerability and rawness and open-heartedness.

How blessed we are, how loved we are in equal measure,

that everything we need for our undoing is served to us so faithfully on the platter of life.

What would we not walk through again and again for the beauty of these sacred moments that all of us on this incredible journey know so well?

"What could you not accept, if you but knew that everything that happens, all events, past, present and to come, are gently planned by One whose only purpose is your good?"

~ *A Course in Miracles*

Denying the Reality of Darkness

February 3

Darkness continues to arise in all its varying forms and parade in front of us. And in a nanosecond, we can be swept up in judgment of others, self-judgment, lack, comparison, depressive or angsty feelings, confusion. All having one common denominator—the simple negativity of mind.

If we have spent much time delving into and releasing suppressed emotions, and the gravitational pull into mind is not intense, then we are in the perfect position to act boldly and to deny the reality and truth of what is appearing. To get behind or above the mind and see it for what it is: an endless display of thought, feeling, sensation seeking, grasping, averting, continuously trying to convince that there is something to fix, something to make better.

Act boldly, as all the great sages have done. Be a sage.

Hand back all the nonsense to your Holy Self. And rise. An uncompromising, vertical rising. The strength and stirring of Truth.

Where is the negativity now? Only blankness, fullness and that certitude that this is all that is real.

Over and over again, we come to see that the ego's only power lies in its capacity to make us believe it's real. Without belief in it, it's just a fizzled out, stale, lifeless bunch of nothing.

But the Love that sources all now begins to shine more steadily through the dream, and the dreamer—blessed creature—nestles more assuredly and trustingly into the arms and safety of Holy Mother God.

A Forgiveness That Awakes

February 7

The worldly forgiveness that we are all familiar with calls on us to forgive someone for what we believe they have done to us. And at certain levels of maturity this is crucial—and beautiful in the relief and peace it brings to our hearts.

And now, so many of us have reached the stage where an even higher order of forgiveness is being called for. We activate this deeper forgiveness by using all the circumstances that trigger us to remember that WE made the whole thing up. Any feeling of being perpetrated on or unfairly treated is coming straight out of our own unconscious minds.

When we are triggered, it is very helpful to ask, *what does this display of phenomena say about me, what does it prove about me?* It is always some variant of unworthiness or unlovability. Always.

And this unworthiness and self-attack is ALREADY INSIDE, and it has no choice but to splash itself out in relationships and circumstances.

What do we do with this belief in unworthiness that keeps displaying itself?

We hold the pain that accompanies it, AND we remember that it is arising out of our pain and guilt from the seeming separation from God. We remember that it is not real because separation never happened.

And this is where we need to bring our attention. Back to where it all began. Back to the recognition that we are the dreamer of the dream, and all these characters, including our own, are figments of our imagination and our attempt to be out on our own, doing our own mad thing. The gods are smiling when we can stand here as the dreamer, taking full responsibility for what we have made.

From here we can hand the whole thing back to our Holy Self, forgive these characters we have willfully made up to do our bidding, and we can forgive ourselves for ever innocently wanting to be separate from our Creator and One Source.

And we come to rest, yet once again, in the quietness of Truth, behind the scenes of hallucination and imagination.

This is the forgiveness that awakes.

Rising in the Light Together

February 13

When we rise up in the Truth, we don't just rise for ourselves. We rise for everybody in pain and suffering, for all that believe it is real. For all who cling to a mistaken identity.

As Jesus said, "You were with me when I arose."

Is there any more beautiful joining than this: the recognition and feeling that our freedom brings, carries, affects all our brothers and sisters in one giant upliftment?

Whatever breakthrough you have today, remember you bring us all with you, closer and closer to our beautiful, collective Homecoming.

Do It with God

February 21

Any feeling of guilt you have in your everyday life is arising out of the overwhelming guilt you felt on finding yourself separate from your Creator.

All the distractions and "self-defeating" behaviors that fall into the mind's category of unholy and carry with them these niggly feelings of guilt and wrongdoing: these are pure pearls in the reclaiming of your innocence.

Even as your aliveness grows and your heart expands, these behaviors and habits of energy can continue. They are the effects of a traumatized nervous system from past emotional experience, and the great unwinding of your nervous system takes time. It takes the time it takes.

The spiritual ego is always wanting to steer you in the direction of "pure" living, but the nervous system knows only how to behave and respond in certain, habitual ways.

So… eat whatever you're eating, drink whatever you're drinking, smoke whatever you're smoking, social media yourself into kingdom come. But, do it with God. Whatever it is, do it with God.

Bring God into the experience. Let yourself be held in a cocoon of presence. God in you, God in the food—there is no separation. And it all becomes soft and gently rounded out. Like a tender stroking of the character, of the child that lives in the character and the nervous system, that never received the love and patient presence it needed. Now, you love yourself like you have never been loved, with great understanding and compassion for the origins of what you seem to have no control over.

The only power "self-defeating" behaviors have is in their capacity to make you feel wrong. So, in bringing in acceptance and gentleness, you turn the ego on its head. The ties of guilt that bind you are unwound and you return, with a grateful heart, to your innate innocence and wholeness.

Being Touched

February 27

Let whatever touches you, touch you. Touch you deeply. And touch you some more. It is the beautiful sensitivity of your heart that had to be fenced in and shadowed over, growing up in an unconscious world.

And now it is opening… opening… the floodgates are opening in surprising eruptions of emotion that connect you once again with the sweetness and inclusiveness of your child heart, your eternal goodness.

The Heart is coming alive and recognizing its own people—only everybody and everything in existence. A joyous reunion with what has laid dormant throughout time, your very own nature of Love.

The Way Out

March 8

The way out is to look calmly at what you're trying to get out of. To LOOK at it.

Be assured that what you're looking at is not you. It's a program. A loopy, repeating, recycling program of lack, victimization, self-attack. Around and around it goes, but it's all laid out so linearly that you forget you've been here a thousand times before.

The singular goal of the program is for the program to stay running, to keep you stuck in the glue of separated consciousness. Often, often, it will look like you can't get out of it. That there is no hope. And this too, no matter how seductive it is, has to be seen as part of the quicksand of mind. It wants to pull you down and in. This is how it is assured of continuity.

Step outside of it. The loopy, painful thoughts may continue but you stay calm, outside. And gradually the calmness takes over—your place of shelter, your place of truth.

One more round of ego versus truth has completed itself, and you stand firmer, lighter and more done with the madness and futility of ego.

Your Heart

March 13

Your Heart, your Holy Self is locked onto you in great love, 24/7, through eternity. The Heart never takes its eyes, its attention, off of you. You are the object of its adoration.

It is so incredibly irrelevant what you do. You think accomplishment gives you value, makes you worthy of love. It is an awful joke, an incredible hoax.

You stand, walk, sit in love all the day long.

Oh, to receive this, dear hearts.

Don't Wait 'til the End of the Conversation

March 21

My stockbroker called this morning, and even though it was a pleasant conversation with some humor and laughter, it wasn't until the end of the interaction that I remembered who he is.

Eternal Beingness, Light, Unending Joy, Perfect Love.

And I forgot who I was: the same.

Our interaction in Truth had so little to do with stocks and bonds and worldly decisions. It was all just an opportunity for true joining. Do we RECOGNIZE each other? Do we remember we are the unchangeable same? Are we blessing each other in this brief moment of connection?

A suggestion to myself and to all of us is "don't wait 'til the end of the conversation." May the Truth appear in the first instant of connecting with our brother or sister. Let's be selfish; let's use each other to remember who we are.

God Tears Everywhere

April 5

I hear the sound of my daughter emptying the dishwasher in the kitchen downstairs, and I am reminded that what the physical senses report is not real. Sounds and smells and sights, all of it, none of it real.

And in this, there arises such a wealth of love and gratitude for the dearness of it all. The sweet familiarity of the small details of these lives we live, from day to day, from year to year.

Recognizing illusion as illusion and Reality as changeless—there is a suspension that happens, and there is nothing empty in it. Such sweetness that springs forth, and we find God in the sounds and God in the sights and God tears everywhere.

Oh, what moments and lives we live when true vision takes the place of the drab of routine.

An Oasis of Love for Yourself

April 13

When you remember that you—the character, body, person—are the ego's secret object of its own hatred for itself, you realize the necessary and transformational capacity of self-love.

God is Love. Ego as opposite—always opposite—is hatred in its most dense form. The incredible fear, guilt, self-hatred that the ego experienced on separation was too much to bear, and a universe of projection came into being. The mind's collective burden now fragmented out into more bearable portions, each individual mind having its own load.

And the ingenuity of projecting out our self-aversion onto family, friends, groups, races came into play.

Every thought, feeling of dislike, judgment toward other is a futile arrow of energy attempting to go out but it goes nowhere. Ideas leave not their source. They just sit in your own consciousness and are really all directed at you. Only you.

It's time to bring it all Home. Let us start a campaign of self-love so our dream world becomes an extension of this love rather than a projection of self-aversion.

When I feel any mind-body disturbance, I love to place both hands over my heart and recite "I love you" several times. It steadies and calms. It is an invitation into the completeness of my own being. It opens up a small oasis of heart presence.

Love is loving the one that seems to be having thoughts and feelings of separation, loving the wounded, conditioned child of my heart, loving the crazed one that believed separation was ever a good idea. Love loving it all, the disturbance, the tight sensations, the angst—how it all seems so fine and benign in the softness of love.

As long as we believe in a person, a doer, shall we not just love the dickens out of it and enjoy an emerging, new world of gentleness, kindness, intimacy with all? A hand-over-heart world.

Looking for Worth

April 19

Our infinite worth was guaranteed by God in the moment of our Creation. There is nothing, nothing that can ever be added to or subtracted from it. It is inviolate, complete, eternal. We live and die in countless lives, and this worth is untouched by any of it.

Looking for worth in the constantly shifting panorama of dreams is painful and absurd. And it is what we do, such dear, lost creatures of time that we think we are. Seeking value in what we do, in who we know and are close to, in personality traits approved of, in our place in the pack. But it never satisfies or fills us up. We are threatened by every twist and turn of circumstance and mind.

Stand tall in a worthiness built on rock, a lighthouse of truth that just shines and shines, a Light that never falters or dims. And let the waves of unworthiness take shelter in your great heart, softened and eroded by countless visitations of pain and tears.

You are the Rock. You are the Light. And all else has no meaning.

Thank You for Helping Me

April 30

This is a pointer from the spiritual teacher Matt Kahn that I have been practicing recently and finding invaluable.

Whenever you find the mind bracing against, irritated or troubled by a thought, person, circumstance, you remember to say, "Thank you for helping me."

Because indeed, it is all helping you. It's the phenomenal display of what you haven't found peace with yet.

Thank you for helping me.

Notice how in one holy instant, the resistance of mind drops away, and the heart moves to connect and join with the grievance, a movement of gratitude, of appreciation, of true seeing. The whole experience softens, and you no longer feel separate and in defiance of what is appearing. It's a movement of consciousness, of heart—towards—rather than away from.

Gratitude for the Heart's reinterpretation of what the mind has made up.

Sometimes, you say "thank you for helping me" to something, and you find your body contracting. The body is not quite able to go there, perfectly demonstrating how some old energetics are keeping the separation going. Then this is a perfect moment to gently receive the contractions in the body. Holding space for, thanking it for continuing to free itself and you.

Thank you for helping me.

Gratitude is the love in our hearts being lived. And here we rest.

Loving our Ancestral Unconsciousness

May 9

Most of us were born into unconsciousness. At the moment of conception, our parental and ancestral heritage became our own. The energetics of survival, war, famine, domination and God knows what became ours. This is what we are the product of, as karmic human beings.

At a certain point in our spiritual maturation, it becomes clear that we are releasing, purging the baggage of centuries—all of it moving through our bodies and nervous systems at the rate and pace of which, thank goodness, we are not in charge. It is experienced as a giant wearing down. As a nameless restlessness, as sickness, as addictive impulses, as relentless emotional triggering. It is the intensity of the awakening process.

Compassionately being a presence for the energetics in your body is the deepest honoring of your ancestors. In holding your body, you hold them all. As Light appears now, it travels effortlessly down the hallways of time, embracing, enlightening all the cries of suffering, calling them in home.

Rejoice in the wearing down. I must say it again, rejoice in the wearing down. Because the wearing down and the rising in Truth are one movement. And the beauty that awaits and lives in your tender, brave heart is golden beyond measure.

You are strong, and it is strength you want and strength you have and strength You are. The strength to hold and love and free it all.

Love Heals and Disperses All

May 16

Separation is imagination. If there is someone you feel shut down to, separated from, know that this experience is not real or true.

It is part of your cloud of illusion, and yes, within that cloud there are energetic walls that are awaiting dissolution so that the love that binds you both is known and experienced all the way through.

Meanwhile, remember that there is in truth, always and only, a straight arrow of love between your heart and the heart of the one you feel disconnected from. Just remembering this can sometimes soften the spell and allow the cloud to blow gently away on the breeze of Truth.

You are Love, they are Love, and Love heals and disperses all.

A Hand Will Come

May 22

The ego is an abuser. This may sound harsh or exaggerated but the closer you come to seeing the core dynamics of ego, the more it's known that this is so.

It is not your friend, and not only does it not have your best interests at heart, but it will run you into the ground, over and over again, and think nothing of it nor have one ounce of compassion for what is being experienced.

It is a program of self-attack and lack: lack of happiness, lack of love, of financial ease, of health. Seeking and never finding. It is everything God is not.

There is no end to the suffering and punishment the ego demands and calls for. We are all too familiar with the feeling of self-sabotage, or the fear that if something is finally going well, it will go belly up at some point. This is the karmic program, based on inadvertent separation from God, collective guilt over our newfound state… and when we feel guilty, we punish ourselves. All unconsciously.

How do we step out of this program? And has our dream become the reflection of Heaven, of love and goodness and wholeness?

We watch it. We disidentify from it. We give it back to our Creator, at moments with the passion of a soul that is done with suffering and has seen through its sordid game. We choose our true identity.

It may not always feel like you have a choice when the blanket of ego feels heavy and dark. But you call out from under the blanket, calling out to God, to Love. Choosing the strength of Christ, of Shiva, of the one eternal Light.

A hand will come, will always come, for we are never left alone and comfortless. And slowly, gently, a vision of a different world appears before our weary eyes, where circumstances convene to meet all needs, where brightness and happiness become our default and life is lived in What We Are and not from what we're not. We are the reflection and extension of God's Love and perfection and nothing—no imaginary somebody, no mad or bad dream—can keep us from this.

As Vigilant as God

June 1

Whatever you're feeling or thinking that is causing disturbance is not real. It is a visitation of energy.

"I can't do it" is a visitation of energy.

"It's too much" is a visitation of energy.

"I'll never come out of this" is a visitation of energy.

Simply contractions. And contractions of feeling and thought are not real, and they are not yours. Because there is no matter, and there is no you, no material you.

There is only God. God, God and more God. And nothing outside of This. We start in God, and we finish in God. And that gigantic roundabout or detour we think we're on: what about a great, big hoist back into the neverlands of never having existed at all?

And we stand up tall and strong, erect, eternal. The Easter Sunday of our consciousness.

Time after time, we must be so vigilant for What We Are. As vigilant as God.

Choose This, Now

June 10

All suffering comes from the original pain of separation.

It will look like it's coming from your circumstances or some "flaw" in the person, but this is more of the mesmerism of mind—having you believe that the external environment is the cause of your upset.

It never is. You are never upset for the reason you think.

The external is a very reliable and inexplicably accurate manifestation and representation of what is already stored inside, in your mind.

This is the grace of the external. It leads us back through the alleyways of pain and surrender to the original cause: separation. Past and through our childhood conditioning, past and through any impact and debris from past lives, all simply reflecting the original error.

Here we stand as the dreamer of the dream, looking out at the mad choice that was made for fragmentation and separation. And what we have at our back is beyond description. Let us choose This now. And let the weary, worn out prodigal son—that never could be prodigal—return to Father-Mother-God.

Mother Love

"Loving the self is loving the Self."

~ Robert Adams

June 19

There are spells and phases where it is divine guidance to take our sights off the ultimate goal of Self-realization and just focus on loving our own being. To let it know how deeply loved it is, and in this the ego can actually let go.

You're allowing Love to come in, and you're allowing it to come in to the place where it is most needed. Your whole world arose out of rejection of self. It arose to take you out of the pain of rejection of self for the heinous crime of separation that never happened at all.

And you find that it is so much larger than love for the child-mind, the personal being; it is a Love that starts to flow from a limitless Heart, and it extends its gentleness to all it sees and touches and handles and holds. It extends to all who cross its now loving, inclusive mind. It is Beauty itself.

It is everything you've ever longed for but thought it couldn't be inside "plain, old" you.

And even as the triggers to the personal self continue, it is now Mother who holds her child, the neglected, the abused, the unloved one—all the children of the Great Heart that greet them at the door of Heaven and call them in.

She is Anandamayi Ma and every Ma. She is Amma, Our Lady, Quan Yin, the Ganga, every name for Mother she is. Her essence is Love that flows and steadfast Presence that stays.

She is the Divine She. And sweet child of Her Divine Heart, she is You. She holds you and waits for you until you are worn down enough that you can let her in and know her as You.

Mother and child. Mother and child. Over and over again, Mother holding, stroking her child until the beautiful, ultimate revelation that there is no child.

Only, ever Mother.

No Ducks in a Row

July 6

Those periods in life when you look around, and everything appears utterly imperfect; all of it feels unresolvable because you've been here so many times before.

Nowhere to turn. No advice to seek. It's been sought too many times already, and lamentation has lost its allure because too much truth is already known.

These are our golden moments, handpicked so astutely by the Beloved who wants us more than our hearts can know. The Beloved cares nothing about us having all our ducks in a row. He and She only want us to see through this mind-made, man-made world of time and space. A cosmos arising from a thought of separation can never be other than highly imperfect.

Your Holy Self loves to have you in this place where even one movement into thought is painful.

Eureka. Surrender to the Inside. Where the Kingdom of Heaven is. Right here, right Now.

And gradually the perfection of Inside takes over and seeps into the "imperfect panorama." And now it's all buoyed up and lightened by the grace of true vision. No issues, no problems, only extending peace and well-being.

And you realize more deeply that any investment in your external ducks is only your enslavement. Now you are His, and now, at last, you can work for Him.

How Does God See Me?

July 12

Do you think God sees you as a bundle of ineptitude, a spiritual failure or whatever brand of self-rejection your mind might be throwing your way today?

God sees only the fruit of his own Heart. His perfect, perfect Child.

He knows nothing of weird fantasies and universes of separation. His singular Love just flows and flows and flows, an eternity of Love and Flow. We sit in this Flow, every inch of us embraced and infilled with this miraculous gentleness.

Let this humble request, "How does God see me?" wake you up out of the stupor of wrongness and into the brand new, yet ancient, realization of the bright light that you are. Wholly innocent. Only God's perfection filling every part.

Taking Ourselves Off the Hook

August 1

Separation is not pretty, and expecting it to be so is more of the folly.

Separation does what it was made to do. Separate. From others, from ourselves, from Love. Judgment, shut down, attack thoughts, closed heart, inability to wish others well: all of it the nuts and bolts of separation.

A suffering being, a being that does not know the wholeness and happiness of Self, is just not equipped to pull out a magic wand and sprinkle fairy dust and blessings of goodness on others. She is just not equipped. And there is zero benefit from reprimanding her. She needs understanding and compassion.

I am so sorry, sweetheart, for ever taking you on this painful ride of separation. I am so sorry. Please forgive me.

And she needs the truth. That the character, the mind is locked into a program, a repeating, mechanistic, automatic program of thoughts and beliefs based on the particular stamp of conditioning, all arising out of the belief in separation from God.

It needs to be seen for what it is. Witnessing consciousness sits and watches the show go by. One wretched, less-than-noble thought after the next. None of it yours. Gratefully, thankfully so. The reality of You is going on at this moment even if mind is discordant. The reality of You is taking over and gradually erasing all illusion.

Stand Your Ground

August 12

Scenes and circumstances continue to play out in front of us, their one seeming objective being to convince us there is something wrong with us, that we are unlovable or that we lack, that the love is over there, not here.

Don't be fooled. Stand your ground. It is time to blow this whole, bad dream apart. Recognize whatever you're seeing and reacting to is coming straight out of your mind, a mind that believes it is separate and whose only function is to keep that belief alive.

The scenes are a set-up. They are out to suck you into misery and to prove to you that you are NOT the incredible beauty that You are. You made it all up. This recognition is your lifeline. It is your point of authority over this dream of pain.

I am not denying the incredible amount of self-nursing, holding and releasing of pain that has happened over many years but when you have reached the point of being able to simply witness the shenanigans of ego, it is to honor that with all your heart. And it is a wonderful thing. You have endured countless lifetimes to come to this point.

So, stand your ground. The ground of Self, of Presence, of Light. And let the movie show of separation roll on by. It has no power to touch YOU. Ever.

We Are Innocence and Love

August 21

The fault-finding with the personal self that happens on the surface of consciousness is a reflection of the greater guilt and sense of wrongdoing over the believed separation.

The nit-picky stuff about appearance, weight, "not good enough," compulsions, the "shoulds" and "shouldn'ts"—all wafting up from the deeper belief that your very existence is wrong. That you are wrong at the core because you left God.

Addressing imperfection and self-sabotage at the surface level doesn't work. For the mature student, there is a much, much bigger invitation at play: the invitation to know our innocence through and through. To know that nothing we could ever do could disturb our eternal innocence.

The character is a child of ego. It is responding purely to the laws of the ego that dictate your family and cultural hypnosis, that dictate the particular set of beliefs and habits of energy you carry.

Here is the beauty of what we get to hold—a wayward child

with a mind and movements of its own, moving from frozen, locked-in energies. The spiritual ego will never be able to prod or coax this child into submission. It is crying out for Love—the love that all "frozen children in adult bodies" call out for.

What is asked for is a gentle, non-judgmental witnessing of all states and behaviors that the critical, parental voice wants to be done with. Gentleness. Tolerance. Acceptance. Hand on heart. Stroking. It is all in divine process.

And sometimes we are gifted with the experience of the Heart going towards it, claiming it for itself—going towards it happily, flowing through crumbling walls that just a moment ago seemed so real and impenetrable. This is the wonder of Love, its power and fluidity. Running to embrace with delight and that singular joy that only a reunion is infused with. Souls coming Home. Precious children thawing out in the light of Love.

We are Innocence and Love. All appearing otherwise is just lining up to know the Truth.

I Am the Truth

September 5

I was rereading this morning an account of an ayahuasca journey I did many years ago, and feeling the vibration of truth in it. Here it is for all of us truth lovers. With love.

I AM THE TRUTH

Slowly, Truth moved in, not with a big bang, but soon it was very noticeable.

NOW, the experience of NOW.

Everything, everything appearing in this NOW. Sounds, movements, things happening, bouts of mind conflict, all appearing in this great, BIG NOW, that has depth, depth. Nothing outside it, everything happening within it, and it is ME.

This NOW is the depth of existence itself. Full-Bodied as in the Body of Everything. Containing Everything.

Mind was experienced as a thought starting up… "I wonder if…" Mind then continuing with another thought in response to that thought, followed by a series of thoughts. Following it and having attention go into it was experienced as conflict. A feeling of conflict in this GREAT EASE.

The mind is just CONFLICT. It doesn't matter if it's mind within myself or mind engaging with another, it's all the same: conflict. Engaging with other is engaging with myself. It's all happening in this NOW.

And this series of thoughts was not anything particularly troublesome in general but just the mind bantering within itself, and yet it was experienced as conflict.

I AM THE TRUTH.

I AM THE TRUTH.

I AM THE TRUTH.

This made itself known over and over again. Arising like a pillar of Truth in the midst of mind, over and over. There were waves of mind, slight nausea, angst and then I AM THE TRUTH arising and gradually a falling away of the mind wave.

It felt like a force of Truth emerging like a rocket and mind falling away.

Strategies of mind making themselves known. How mind loves to make plans. Always making plans. Some of the strategies were hard to look at, seeing how the mind wanted to curl into itself, not to be exposed or have to look at the truth of its games.

I imagined speaking to a friend, and suddenly it was seen that the friend didn't exist. The mind's perception of my friend didn't exist. How the mind didn't want to look at that, didn't want to see that it speaks to itself all the time.

Mind is very conditioned in me, as this character Pema, to respond to everything with "I can't" and "It's hopeless." Over and over again, it runs away into this habit of energy. Seen to be just a habit.

It is never about combatting "I can't" with "I can" or "It's hopeless" with "It's not hopeless." It is to see this as a habit of mind, simply not true, not who I am. To wait for Truth to move, if and when it moves.

There was an imperative to SPEAK THE TRUTH, and the habit of "I can't" came in very strong. It was also seen that all the qualifying and justifying of itself that this character does was nauseating. The preamble, the explaining, the trying to soften things for "other minds," trying to be inoffensive, operating in a vibration of constant apology—all experienced as nauseating.

I AM THE TRUTH. SPEAK THE TRUTH.

YOU ARE THE TRUTH. SPEAK THE TRUTH.

Our Divine Throne

September 14

Lies hurt. The lies you tell yourself about who you are hurt. And sometimes they hurt like crazy.

And this is a good thing. Because every one of these spells has the miraculous component of giving you an extra push back into the Truth of what you are. Into True Life, with no interface with the bundle of lies we've taken on. Just the pure Truth of what you are.

Light. Quietude of Heart. Surety of identity. Sitting on our divine throne. No falling prey to that tidal pull of mind into misery and smallness and weakness.

We are constantly being invited into our grandeur. Grandeur wants us and we want our grandeur. How inevitable is the ending of all bad dreams. Alleluia.

Stay Vertical

September 24

Such tendencies there are to slump down into the problems of the human condition. To let the mind be distracted into trying to figure out ways and means to fix the presenting problem. Always with a dash of *you're doing something wrong. You're wrong.*

Rehashing the same thoughts that you had yesterday, last week, last year. This is all staying on the horizontal plane of linear time and space and suffering and conundrums.

The only answer is to go Vertical. It is rising up to where there is no error. Standing up, divorcing yourself completely from the endless battering of mind.

Stay Vertical. Stay Light. Stay Truth. Stay Perfect.

Again and again, we see the only purpose of the world and all its issues is to push you into remembering its meaninglessness. To push you Vertical.

Be Happy to Shine

October 2

Carry yourself like the amazing Child of God that You are. There is nothing small or shrinking about someone who knows the Truth of their being.

Smallness and shrinking back, as much as you may feel it is unbidden by you, is arrogance. It is the attempt to declare that you are something other than the greatness of God. It is an act of separation and willfulness. Aligning with this small, cramped, limited self just so we could be out on our own, doing our own special, miserable existence.

We are so Big, so Bright, so Beautiful. Each and every one of us, such perfect, delightful creations of God.

So, come on out to the forefront of your own energy, of your own goodness. Ask for what you need and want and what you know in your integrity to be right for you in this moment.

Walk tall with a spring in your step because of who you are. Be happy to shine, to "shine the Light in which you are created." This is our purpose.

Pema in the early 90s

2017

Find Your Good

January 20

I became an American citizen last year, just in time to vote for my love, Bernie. With pride and gratitude and tears in my eyes, I voted for someone who touched my heart with his sense of fairness and all things noble, kind and good.

And strangely today I am again proud to be American. To live in a country and a consciousness that is willing and courageous enough to show its shadow. To have it surface in all its glory. In the arrogance, prejudice and inhumanity that seems to mark our new government.

That marks this mind.

Just as "my own" shadow keeps surfacing and dissolving, the shadow of my adopted country does likewise. My mirror. And all happening inside this mind.

It is all a call for love. And true vision.

Can we look at our brother, Donald, and just for a moment remember who he really is? Bypassing content and appearance, we look beyond to sense and see the Light and Love that animates this charade of separation to see his shining Self. Yes, we can do this because it is simply the Truth, and in doing so, we strengthen that shift in ourselves to know and live out from our true identity.

True vision heals and nurtures Truth and uplifts all. And reminds us separation doesn't work and never will.

Watching the inauguration this morning, my heart erupted in a passionate prayer to Donald Trump. "Please be good. Find your good."

May I, may we all, find our good. The goodness of God, the goodness of our true nature.

Innocence

March 30

A wee hug from my innocence to yours. Same, same.

With Love, Pema

Dear Friends

April 25

Sickness and malaise in the body is, for many of us, a huge catalyst for the softening and humbling of the character that must occur as we simultaneously rise in the Truth of what we are. The wearing down and the rising up in Truth is one movement. One pea in a pod.

From the vantage point of "serious illness," much has been seen here and continues to be revealed and processed. It is very intense at times; it is very challenging, and it is so very beautiful. And some of this I would like to express in words because it is healing for me to be open, and if it serves you in any way, it is a beautiful joining that I am so grateful for.

I live at the moment with a "terminal illness." Stage four cancer—metastasized breast cancer in the bone. It is a huge wake-up call that allows for little indulging in the future or postponement of forgiveness of myself and others.

And there is a demand for standing in the Truth that is so vibrant and intoxicating. A demand for that great transfer of trust from the ego to what really sustains us and lives us: our eternal, holy Self.

Until soon, I trust. I love you all… we are one.

Ever more grateful to be here.

Loving This Human One

May 28

Time and again, our life circumstances bring us back around to the unhealed places in our being, to the ever-deepening unraveling of mind. And the greater the crisis, the more the conditioning is illuminated.

Wherever love is lacking, it can bear a certain kind of bitter fruit. In my case it was breast cancer followed by metastasis to the bone. And it brought me up short, amongst other things, to the simple, tender need of this being to be loved and nurtured.

All we ever really want as humans is to be loved and valued, to not have to bear the pain of the deep soul unworthiness we all carry. I was so focused externally in the pursuit of love and worth, placing others and their needs above my own, reaching out to tend to others to win approval and belonging. An aware, kind, respectful, honoring relationship with myself was not happening. And despite a great amount of soul growth, there still remained so much self-judgment and self-neglect.

However we are with ourselves will always be a replay of childhood experience. And childhood experience is a manifestation of what the soul believes about itself, our karmic totality arising from the believed separation from God.

The hand of mother is our own hand tending to us, reflecting the soft beauty of our hearts or the neglect and unkindness of our unhealed mind.

The voice of father, be it stern and silencing or gentle and guiding, is our own voice echoing up from the deeper chambers of our mind. Our will, the willfulness of separation, is always being done.

But mercifully, the great Correction is always at hand, awaiting our cracking open and permission to move in.

It's about opening to receive God's great Love for us. In Truth, it's what we are, but it can feel dualistic for some time. It feels like a part of us is offering love to the woundedness, but it is really pure Love being allowed to flow through us.

Becoming a sacred companion to yourself is not a quick project. It is a process, and understanding that it is a huge process for everybody will help ward off any arising impatience or sense of failure.

There are some specific ways that have been helping me greatly to let the Love flow more readily into the totality of me:

Noticing the self-reproaching thoughts that arise so often and handing them back to the Beloved who knows their falsity immediately. You just keep handing them over. They are not Yours.

A gentle "I'm sorry for being so hard on you" can help foster greater compassion and connection.

Placing your hand on your heart at odd moments as you go through your day can be a reminder to be gentle and patient with yourself and with everything appearing to you.

Opening to receive God's Love.

Great leniency is called for when it comes to behaviors that you are critical of, or guilt feelings for not being able to take action around things your mind tells you would be beneficial for you. It is not about changing behaviors, and it is certainly not about forcing yourself into taking any kind of action. Having understanding for the wealth of conditioning that doesn't allow us to be good to ourselves… this is our work, and there is such beauty in bringing kindness to all that we are and all that we do. Behaviors change in time as the human starts to reflect the deep Love that is being offered it.

Such a tender homecoming and sense of nourishment in treating and seeing our being as God does.

In my experience this work we do in loving the human one seems to be a preliminary step or at least runs alongside the huge arising in Truth that we are being called to. It is very important work, and we come to see that there is a great difference in separating from the small self, based on conditioning and a lack of love, rather than a dissolving of interest in the character arising from true seeing.

True seeing is that you are as God created you. The Light. The great Love. And only that. That there is no human one and never has been. There is no physical, material body, no character, no person. But until all that we have made in error is folded into the great Heart, it will pull us out into the misery of the dream.

I love you. We are One.

2018

Grateful to Share with You

July 31

Dear friends,

Such a long time since I've been in touch. Navigating the world of sickness has kept me pretty quiet and secluded. It has been a time of great challenge, but the spiritual rewards that this passage offers are profound and beautiful.

On a practical, bodily level, I have Stage Four breast cancer with metastasis to the bone. Late last summer, it seriously looked like I was dying. But the body rallied, and now, a year later, I am still here. I get around slowly, driving a bit, cooking, participating in life to a certain degree.

On the level of the divine, I am so perfect, untouched by any of this. I do not have sickness, and this I lean into and own with as much vigilance as is available in any moment.

One of the gifts of this time has been the experience of an extreme sense of vulnerability. Not being able to function combined with the feeling of fragility and debilitation seems to open organically into the vulnerability that lies dormant in us all. There have been so many tears, an unprecedented amount of tears, releasing, releasing and most of the time not even knowing what was being let go of.

But the arising of Love in the midst of and on the coat-tails of this vulnerability was undeniable. Nature's heart-opening ways.

The dearness of all form makes itself known—the longing to wrap your arms around anything and everything that appears. What grace it all is to feel Yourself burst through the walls of separation, to join, to bless and wish-oh-so-well. The slightest touch of God's presence as in a kindness received or perceived just splices the heart open in deepest gratitude and recognition. The goodness and innocence of all beings begins to shine through the prior overlay of mind, of judgment and grievance. In these moments and spells, the status of the body seems so irrelevant.

There has also been ample time to sit with and feel into the fear of dying. This primal fear of ungroundedness, of not being in this familiar body I identify with as "me." Of going off into the ethers someplace, untethered, nothing to hang on to. Conceptually, I knew this fear wasn't real, but the body had another experience with its agitation and jitteriness. Sitting with this was invaluable, knowing that the first step in transcending fear is allowing it to surface to consciousness.

And paradoxically, at other moments, noticing how attracted to death this mind is: seeing it as the only way out of a challenged, compromised body, as the most convenient thing. But the words of *A Course in Miracles* ring in my ears with their Self-reminding power. "This world is not left by death but by Truth." I love this Truth, and to this I am being carried.

Grateful to be here, to share myself with you.

All Love, Pema

Retreating from Body Malaise

August 10

There are times when you just have to stop wishing and wanting the body to feel better. When you must retreat, so to speak, to the backdrop of all phenomena.

To the mind, this is so not attractive. Remember that what the ego wants, its sole *raison d'etre,* is to survive as a separate entity and to be comfortable enough as this. It cannot help but offer a certain amount of discomfort as unhappiness and lack is the law of ego, the natural outpicturings of the separated state. But it doesn't want too much discomfort as this is what forces the hand of separation and creates the longing to burst out of it.

"Too much discomfort" can be a great thing.

So, we go against the mind when we retire to the Truth. And there's nothing like the inability to fix body malaise to force this step. When all resolution inside the dream fails, we move back.

And this is a holy moment. A pure, undiluted movement of consciousness. The divine plan of our lives in action.

It is surrender. It is resurrection.

And how peaceful it is here. Just plain peaceful. Not necessarily any bells and whistles or blissed out states. Just that nice, quiet, centered feeling in your heart. And this is finally all that is real.

How incredibly blessed we are that we have Home to come to, that we are Home. We are simultaneously the prodigal son and the Son that never left. What perpetual grace.

A Brother Smiles Upon Another

August 30

"A brother smiles upon another, and my heart is gladdened."

This is a line from *A Course in Miracles* that has stood out for me over the years. I never thought I would reach the place where the sentiment evoked in this beauty could rise in my being.

With an ego construct burdened by beliefs in "not important" and "left out of the love," it seemed far-fetched to think that the day could come when I could witness a favored friend or special one engage and commune with another and not feel that familiar angst and agitation of mind.

But we keep doing our work, meeting the pieces that life never fails to expertly dole out, going in and out of the "karmic car wash," as a friend of mine aptly called it recently.

And to your great surprise, one day you find yourself looking at a scene, or hearing something that never failed to upset you and there is no reaction. And it is a neutrality and non-reactiveness that feels like a quiet slice of Heaven because of what has come and gone for years, decades even.

And you realize, you *know,* you could never be left out of the Love. That love being shared before your eyes, only awakens it more in yourself. Love is in the air. We are Love. Feeling left out of it is only experienced in the land of illusion, whose vaporous state we are each brought to see, in our own way, in our own timing.

Thankfully, gratefully, it is so.

"A brother smiles upon another, and my heart is gladdened."

That Edge of Identity

December 12

Suffering will inevitably just push you over that edge of identity. Are you going to continue subscribing to being weak and powerless, a victim, needing love, OR are you going to step back and claim what you know to be true? You are eternal, God-infused Love, Light, at the mercy of nothing.

One is a crushing program of suffering, of self-punishment, of believing (in my case) that physical death will end this program. It won't. Nothing will end the experience of limitation except a total shift in identity where your innocence and beauty is not up for grabs because nothing else can even feature there.

I bow to What I am, and I simultaneously rise in Who I am. And gratitude prevails.

2019

At the Threshold of Home

January 11

The time comes when you realize the only function this life dream has is to see how much it can sway you away from Reality. Its vacuum suction power is dwindling. Its endless attempts to make you believe something and everything is important are losing their fizz.

What grace to stand here at the threshold of Home, to sit in the ante-chamber of heaven, to view the landscape of that oh-so-significant story of you with a body, and all the other bodies and characters that people your life.

Not without some tears perhaps, as your love for all of it flows more easily now, not without some regrets that you bid it goodbye in a certain way, but you know you've made it all up and that all these beings you love so dearly are very well. Eternally well. And you know there is a Love at your back that transcends even this precious, delicious, personal feeling of love.

What grace to no longer see with the body's eyes. What grace to know the Light of God is our inheritance. What grace it is to come on in home.

Ground Down to Pure Love

January 19

That feeling of separation from another. Of judgment, distance, not being open. How uncomfortable it is now when the littleness of the heart has shown itself so clearly. And paradoxically, it also seems to disturb less as we remember there is no ownership. It is not ours to fuss with. Just a mechanical, totally reliable program, primed to react in the same old, same old ways. Never a new trick.

We let the discomfort be here. We no longer deride ourselves for its presence. We are in the last frontiers of separation now, so what matter these trailing threads of mind, of belief in difference.

Perhaps the discomfort wants to cry itself out, releasing into the warmer climes of the heart. And as it all mercifully softens again, we are blessed with true sight.

Who is this one but our savior, our true friend? The one who is showing us where we are still removed from Love (but never really). And he is the one who points us back there, ever lighter, ever deeper, ever more open.

And now we greet our friend anew, not afraid to love or show we care. How soft their appearance when we have learned to look past false appearance. To see the friendly face of the Beloved, as it always was but our eyes were too dimmed before to see.

We all tread so bravely on this pilgrimage to the Heart. Being ground down to pure Love. No matter the frequent lamentations of mind, would we ever really have it any other way?

Being Inside the Mind

February 13

This is an account of a deep shamanic journey I had years ago. It has been moving through my consciousness this past week supporting me greatly in this ongoing dis-identification from the mind.

The journey began with an experience of being squeezed down, suffocated, with every thought being taken away from me and left as nothing.

And then, I found myself in a lot of space, but I didn't know where I was or what was going on. With surprise, I noticed an aspect of Divine Mother was with me. There was no fear here, and I realized I was outside the mind, in Reality, and there was great peace and ease.

I noticed a tiny speck of black dust in the far distance, and Mother informed me that was the mind. Suddenly I found myself back in absolute turmoil. So uncomfortable. And with a thudding *oh no,* I realized I was back in the mind. I was in the heart of feelings, underneath what we know as our everyday feelings, tears, etc.

Mother kept telling me to "Look, look at this," but it was all so uncomfortable that I was unable to step back and look at anything. At a certain point, she told me, "You're just inside the mind." This made so much sense, unbelievable sense. She began to show me how everything in this world and in my inner states are all "just being inside the mind." Inside that speck of dust.

Incarnations, births, deaths, all the suffering in this world are us "being inside the mind." Black and white, young and old, light and dark, all these differentiations I see are that: *being inside the mind.* The duality of the senses, pleasure and pain, pleasure and distaste. Aversions, jealousies, everything I see and feel.

There was an image of the mind being like a stranded space shuttle, all of us trapped inside, playing out this bizarre, suffering world.

That we are Love made itself known and also how we experience these waves of mind and believe them. It felt like a real awakening (in the moment) to see all of this so clearly.

This past week when discomfort arises, I have been remembering

I am "just being inside the mind," and it brings the contrast of Reality and mind into focus. And something rests again.

We continue in this process, that is a process until it's not. Truth inevitably wins out. Praise God.

A Steady Stream of Thank-Yous

February 25

With enough wearing down, your life frequently becomes a steady stream of thank-yous. You want to kiss and stroke anything and everything in front of you, anything that serves you even in the smallest of ways. A drop of rain on your open hand feels like a blessing.

You sense the interconnectedness of all things and your gratitude weaves its way back, thanking, blessing all the people and steps that made the appearance of this "object" possible. All for you, right here, right now.

And you remember how intense it's been and how this very intensity was the shining path. You're grateful for all the burning and erosion. For gossiping indulged in, the condemnation of yourself and others, the one-upmanship and one-downmanship. For physical malaise and dysfunction, loss of body image, the not knowing if you're living or dying. The specialness craved at every turn because, sweet being, you didn't know you were Love itself.

The pain of forgetting becomes the remembering.

And what it all erodes down to is so beautiful, you can't believe you've lived a whole lifetime without this in view. How could we have ever chosen to live the misery of separation? And yet we did, dear foolish souls that we are. And all only in imagination.

The beauty of Love, of true life, eternal sunshine on your face. It beckons to us all, so lightly and yet so wholeheartedly. And its name is Home.

"Trailing clouds of glory do we come from God who is our home: Heaven lies about us in our infancy."

- William Wordsworth

And always. Throughout time. And through eternity.

All or Nothing

March 22

It really is all or nothing. Identification is such. You're either an apple or a banana. You're either the eternal Self, the shining Light, or you're the separate mind.

These two can never meet. We will never, ever find wholeness in this dream of utter fragmentation. But it's certainly not for want of trying, and at some point, we must stop toiling and thrashing around in this parody of life looking for Life.

With every disturbance we have a royal invitation to rise up above the battlefield or to withdraw back to awareness. Whichever way works for you. You're either this vertical force that can look down on the fray or you're resting in the background as a clear witness and presence.

This must become everything you want. There is nothing subtle about this.

With every niggling thought and wrinkle in the mind, with every surge of intensity, it must become paramount to ask yourself: *Where am I standing? Where am I located? Where am I looking from? Am I in the Truth or am I lost in the bubble of mind, that bouncing show of duality that does nothing but bounce around?*

Let your whole existence be about this. Cling to Reality. Focus on the Light that you are. It is the only reason we are here. It is all or nothing.

The reward is the end of suffering. It is the joy that bubbles up from your creator and infuses the life dream. And you feel a heart connection with everyone you think of and every dear brother that crosses your path, a path that was always divine, but now you feel it and know it.

Pure life. Divine life. Intimate life.

I Am a Miracle

April 4

When we make these large statements, we are never speaking of the ego-character. We speak of the Truth of who we are. To the ego, this is the height of arrogance and self-glorification, but to the Self, it is cause for great rejoicing. Another one of her dear children saying goodbye to the misery of false identification and cleaving a sure path home to Her.

A miracle is God's creation. A light-filled being that knows nothing of malice or suffering or bodies or form. Spun from eternal gold, unchanged from the moment Love created it like itself.

I am a miracle. It makes this body stand up straighter, head raised to my Creator, who ironically dwells within. Something brightens, a feeling of aliveness, tears of recognition spring forth. I feel like light dancing on water, and for a few moments I am home.

You are a miracle. Hear the truth about Yourself. Let us be done with the never-ending foolish and frantic fantasies.

All those false self-images. Let us look past these deceptive body appearances and see this same Truth in everyone and everything. Light dancing on water. God's offspring everywhere, without gender or form. To be without a body, to see beyond the body is to be in our natural state.

We are a miracle. Stand up tall, proclaim the truth and be your sparkly Self. Everything in the heavens has your back, the sages and masters of all time rejoicing wholeheartedly with you.

You Can't Do Anything Wrong

April 8

You can't do anything wrong. It's all such a set-up. An incredibly seductive set-up. We have these ingrained rules and laws which if we break, the mind becomes merciless.

This morning I was watching something holy online, and the thought came of wanting to text someone. *Oh no, can't do that now—that's not respectful of the sacredness...*

And thankfully I had a flash of truth—*you can't do anything wrong*—there is no wrong. It is all illusion. There is no world, no sacredness, no text. Such a sense of lightness.

It doesn't matter one iota what the so-called "wrongdoing" is. It's all a hoax. An incredible hoax as the film critic Roger Ebert saw on his death bed. It is to see the ego dynamic of "making you wrong." This is how it snags you, keeps you bound in the misery. It can be so convincing.

It all stems from the tremendous feeling of guilt and pain that we experienced when we believed we separated from God. Guilt is our middle name and we project that out onto the myriad ways we believe we're doing something wrong. It starts inside. Guilt and pain find their way to make you feel guilty and miserable.

For example, if you feel bad about eating the "wrong" foods, it has nothing to do with the food. The guilt is present in the mind FIRST and gives rise to the circumstances. It is not the other way around, as we all too naturally believe. Projection makes perception.

The tendency of mind is to dwell on the wrongdoing. If you could just eliminate that, all would be well with your life. And then here we are, endlessly parading around at a certain level of consciousness that will never, ever bring resolution.

We have to be bigger than this. We ARE bigger than this. We have to start seeing through the smartness of the ego.

It's never about specifics or changing behaviors. It's about bringing any sense of wrongness to the Beloved. Bringing that long-buried guilt and darkness to the Light that you are. Handing it over, the Light knows what to do with it.

We are perfect. Perfectly innocent. Always doing just the right thing. How wonderful it would be to go through our days imagining the Beloved stroking our sweet heads and reminding us in every moment how beautiful and innocent we are and how every movement we make is so blessed and loved and adored. The ultimate endorsement of Light and Love. It is how it is in Truth.

Our Perfect, Shining Innocence

April 21

Such mercy flowing towards us all the time. Incredible mercy and love and whatever quality it is that lets us know that we are innocent, through and through.

We were created innocent and despite our meanderings into this crazy, mortal dream spawned by the collective guilt and pain of separation, we are undisputedly, always and forever innocent. This whole, physical universe is a figment of our imagination, and nothing ever did happen.

When we think of innocence we think of puppies and kittens and babies cooing; young ones dancing and playing; old, infirm ones who seem to have lost their rigid defenses, and are no longer threatening. They tug at our hearts, drawing us into their wonder. Their innocence is delightful and wakes up our own.

However, we don't feel innocent in our everyday lives. We feel bad about all the fault-finding, the nitpicking of others, of ourselves. But the others are just images we made up, and all the thoughts about them are only telling us what we think of ourselves. And the negativity towards ourselves, when you begin to see straight after a lot of unraveling, is much ado about nothing. How often we need to remind ourselves of this: it is much ado about nothing. It doesn't matter what you think you've done or not done in this dream. It's a DREAM. All the enactments of a thousand, imagined lifetimes cannot even touch our true identity.

The ego is like a dark, heavy coat we wear, and it makes no difference whether we're wearing it or if it's half-off or off—our innocence is always there shining underneath.

The last judgment, the last pronouncement is that we never did leave Home. Its shining is our shining, its light, our light. We are enfolded in it and from it; we can never part.

The Beauty of Blessing

May 16

There is a wonderful lesson in *A Course in Miracles* that is so good to take to heart and to take with you through your day:

"My holiness blesses the world."

The invitation is to bless everything in sight, in mind; indeed, they are the same. To go through your day saying to everyone you meet, *"My holiness blesses you."* Quietly inside.

And I love to add, "Your holiness blesses me."

It bypasses the mind's usual fascination with form, appearance and personality and takes you right to the heart of the matter—your essence meeting their essence. It lifts you into Truth and reinforces regularly that you and they are indeed Holy. That you are Light. That you are Peace. Whichever aspect of non-ego presence that carries a transmission for you and makes your heart lift up.

My Light blesses you. Your Light blesses me. To see the Light in your brother is to see the Light that shines within you. It establishes your true identity and theirs.

You can bless your food, your home, objects, thoughts, other drivers on the highway. You have your whole world to bless, and what a wonderful oyster it is. Sometimes, something as simple as a blessing can eclipse a trigger or judgment. You don't always have to go through the whole process of evaluating what this person is triggering in you. If the mirroring process is still rather new to you, you may need to bring your projections back home and see what beliefs are creating the particular scenario. Or if there is much pain and turmoil, this needs to be tended to, of course. But so many of us now are ego war veterans, and we know our own mind well and can see easily that everything we react to has a well-worn path that always funnels down to one or two core beliefs—always some form of unworthiness or lack, or your specialness getting crumbled in some way.

As you concentrate on blessing instead of focusing on the irritation, there may be a corresponding stir in the heart, and you find yourself wanting to move towards others rather than away, you want to look in their eyes, you want to hug them and tell them how beautiful they are. In the grace of Truth filling your system, this beauty is all you can see and feel right now. A meeting of souls, a joining in Love.

I have found this to be a potent practice and the Light just grows and grows. It is what we are. How can it not show its presence more when we nurture it? Every time that you are blessed to feel the effects, you recognize this IS the happy dream. These moments are the real world.

"There is a Light in you which cannot die, whose presence is so holy that the world is sanctified because of you."

~ A Course in Miracles

What You Wish Another, You Wish Yourself

May 20

I was forty years old when I first took stock of the "maliciousness" of this mind. It had been there all along; I just didn't have enough self-awareness to recognize it, to take in what it meant.

I was in great suffering at the time. My husband had been diagnosed with an aggressive brain cancer, and we, as a family, were reeling in shock and turmoil. My young daughter had a friend whose baby brother was quite sick, and there were fears he might have meningitis. As I listened to my daughter on the phone with her friend, I realized I wanted this baby to have meningitis. I wanted this other family to suffer like I was suffering.

It was rather horrifying for me in the moment to see this, which is why I remember exactly where I was, standing at the kitchen sink washing dishes.

This particular flavor of separation, of not being able to wish certain others well, was a cause of great turmoil for me for many, many years. At moments I felt like I was the lowliest soul in the universe. It was most active with people that I felt envious of. There was some inward satisfaction, something appeased in hearing about another's difficulty.

Through the years, there were several responses that helped enormously.

The first one was acknowledging the nature of these thoughts to others, in the spirit of "no private thoughts." Sharing with teachers and friends who understood well the mechanics of ego and were totally unfazed by any confessions of hatred. As I spoke more, I came to see I was not alone in these ego devices. After all, we are one collective mind.

I also began to give these thoughts back to God. I had no control over their arising, none at all. No admonishment of self did anything. It only heaped angst on the original dilemma. I learned that it was so fine not to want these thoughts, not to want separation. At one point, I chose separation but now gratefully, gratefully in every moment, I could choose again. I could pray to have only the loving thoughts of God.

As I matured more, I was also able to take in that these thoughts and feelings meant nothing. Zilch. They are an ego device but there is no ego, and reacting to them only kept them real. Alleluia. What a blessing. Ignoring the ego is how we dispel it. It survives and thrives on attention and reaction.

These thoughts still arise at moments but I can thankfully say they don't disturb very much. Their demise feels inevitable. More and more it is realized that what I wish another, I wish myself. There is only One here. I gently shift it all to a blessing—blessing the thought, blessing the person, blessing myself. I sit back and let the goodness of God come in as it always does, in its own perfect timing.

Illusion Free

May 27

Waking up this morning feeling dopey as I'm wont to do at this time, I look out the window at the day, and uncomfortable thoughts of how my life is arise. Thoughts of dullness, of struggle in this body, of not having a "proper" life because of sickness. This so familiar story rising in the mind.

But something is different. The yucky thoughts don't have the strength, the binding force they once did. A sensing of Light, of presence, of something spacious, vaporous, undefinable is here too. Ah yes… of course… this is life. This is what it's all about.

Pure grace. What can one do? Only bow to the almighty in gratitude, in relief born from years and years of believing the wrong, miserable thing.

Thank you, Father, for creating me as You. Eternal. Unchanging. Illusion-free. This zone of reality where dreams of being a body and a self could come and bind and grossly entertain but never could unseat the real.

"You are as certain of arriving home as is the pathway of the sun laid down before it rises, after it has set, and in the half-lit hours in between. Indeed, your pathway is more certain still. For it cannot be possible to change the course of those whom God has called to Him."

~ *A Course in Miracles*

A Holy Encounter

June 11

This morning I called my pharmacist. As I was waiting on hold, I started silently blessing him.

My holiness blesses you. Your holiness blesses me.

I sensed the Light he is, the Truth of his being that has nothing to do with his everyday human existence. I imagined the other people working with him and their Light shining up the whole room. Before I knew where I was, I was sitting in a pool of kind Light and imagining it extending out to the whole world.

What started out as a mundane telephone call became a holy encounter, another sweet opportunity to deepen my recognition of my Self.

May this become second nature to us. May every meeting become a holy one, and may we spend our days constantly uplifting, illuminating all around us.

"The peace of God is shining in me now."

True Forgiveness Is Exciting

June 17

Scrolling down through Facebook, I come across a photo, and my body tightens up instinctively. I feel that slight discomfort of judgment, of separation. I want to rush to click "Like" and move on. Pretend to myself there is no reaction, nothing a "Like" cannot gloss over and smooth out.

But somehow, Grace has me stop this morning and remember that denying the ego's reactions only leaves them fermenting away, and the gap of separation between myself and other lives on in my belief system.

I look at the dislike of other. It is a feeling, a thought of inferiority. Perfect separating material from myself, from other. And in the next breath, it could just as easily be a thought of superiority which is a mask, an overlay on the deep unworthiness and self-hatred that haunts us all. At the core we still believe ourselves guilty of grievous wrongdoing, that we separated from our loving Father.

I let whatever distress is in the body arise and be here. I know that feeling this directly is a shortcut and really good news that it's here. I begin to open to the recognition that this is all happening in mind. Only in mind. All made up by this mind. The possibility of forgiveness starts making itself felt.

Forgiveness may seem like a strange term for what is in process here. It smacks a bit of an old-fashioned Christianity and dualism that not all non-dual seekers can relate to or be interested in. But in the context and teachings of *A Course in Miracles,* it is as non-dual as it gets. It could just as easily be labeled "undoing" or "seeing through the dream."

What true forgiveness means is recognizing over and over that the separation never happened. This is how big this word is, and this is how BIG we are invited to be. To own this Truth.

You forgive another for "what he did not do." How can we possibly say this when it is obvious someone has hurt us? But what is proof of someone doing something to us is proof of us doing something to ourselves.

The picture of someone who triggered my inferiority program is an image that is coming out of my own mind. I made this person up, and all he or she does is represent to a tee what I am already feeling and believing inside. This is the law of the ego, and there is nothing more foolproof than this. Our world is a motion picture of our beliefs.

And everything that hurts is replaying the imagined separation. What a fiasco.

True forgiveness is the most exciting thing we've got. It's where we get to take this expansive jump from believing that the external rules our lives, to the relief of taking responsibility for our reactions. We jump from any notions of victimization and "being unfairly treated" to the power we have to correct.

In my next post I'd love to outline the steps to forgiveness that I've used these past years and that have helped me greatly in letting go of grievances and standing in the Truth, with the help of our Holy Self.

"The holiest place on earth is where an ancient hatred has become a present love."

- A Course in Miracles

Reeling Back Our Projections: Steps to True Forgiveness

June 24

The deeper premise of this forgiveness work is based on the non-dual understanding that this world of form and matter and separation is an illusion of mind. That there is only Oneness—in spirit, not in form. That we have never left our Source, and we but dream this mental dream of judgment, projection, blame and conflict.

I have used these steps in recent years and have found them to be very freeing. The way they are outlined may not necessarily work for you, so feel free to play with them and adjust to your own heart's way. Strong karmic pieces do not move easily, and you may need to repeat these steps many, many times over. Don't think they are not working or that nothing is happening. Each time you do this, you are releasing another layer of illusion and slowly, gradually full release from the world you made is experienced. And the happiness, Love and Light that you are makes itself known and lived in you.

You are learning to forgive your brother for "what he did not do." Because it is all imagined. It has no reality.

When you notice you're triggered by a person or circumstance:

1. You remember this is your dream. You made this up.

(Just saying this slowly to yourself several times over—*I made this up—I made this up*—trying to take it in—you are already half way out of the vise of victim.)

2. What is this making you feel? Irritated, angry, betrayed, bereft, left out of the love or goodness, less than, etc. Determine what you feel and believe.

(These feelings and states of mind are already inside me and are being projected out, making this scenario happen. These beliefs are creating MY dream. I project what's in here, and then I perceive the same. It has NOTHING to do with the person or the event. This part is so important, shifting the source of the disturbance from the external to the internal. Of course, it is challenging at first, but stick with it. The rewards are so great.)

3. You remember where these feelings are coming from.

(Now that you've brought back the projection entirely inside you, you look at the source of the angst. It is all coming from the original, collective guilt and pain of separation from God. It will undoubtedly be replaying events and feelings from childhood, from past lives, and these may well surface and come to mind, but underneath all of that, it is the pain of the loss of Love, the pain of finding ourselves kicked out of Heaven.

I can't tell you how wonderful and clear it is to make this connection. It may start out as an intellectual awareness, but after a while it will become an experience and more easily accessible.)

4. Sit for a while with any contraction that's appearing in the body, any release of emotion that wants to happen. Just keep making the connection between the present pain and the original loss of Father/Mother.

5. Now you give it all back to God, to your Holy Self, to the Holy Spirit. To Ramana, to Jesus, to your heart's favorite sage.

(You hand it over. You don't want separation anymore. You bring the darkness to the Light. You lay it all at the altar of your heart. If you like, you can imagine giving it over into sacred hands of Light. This step is the easiest because your work is done; your Holy Self takes over, and it is actually Spirit that takes care of the undoing. All that was needed was your willingness and intention.)

6. Thank the Holy Spirit for healing your mind.

(This is beautiful to do because again, it is an acknowledgment that He is taking care of it, not you as a self-concept. And it is an acknowledgment that it is being undone; it is already undone. Your brother is innocent, and you are innocent because nothing ever happened. As Roger Ebert pronounced on his death bed, "It is all an incredible hoax.")

I'd love to hear from you and how it goes if you try this.

Time to Stop the Charade

July 3

What if some benevolent, masterful being appeared before us—someone we know understands with compassion the workings of this universe and put this to us:

Who wants to suffer? Hold up your hands those of you who believe you must suffer, those of you who want to suffer, those of you who deep down believe that suffering will mitigate your "sins" and wrongdoing and save you from even greater hardship.

If you are suffering in your life, I'm afraid your hand went up. Mine did.

You of course have no idea on the conscious level of mind that your hand went up, that you asked suffering to come in. Just the opposite: when suffering appears, you are most upset, looking feverishly for the cause. How can this be? And what do I need to do to get out of this?

We are so terribly unaware of what is running in our unconscious minds, underneath the tip of the iceberg. How we actually call everything to us based on these sad beliefs of guilt and undeservability.

God's will for us is perfect happiness. We need to say this a hundred times over and a hundred times over again. Just below the glue, the quicksand of the ego's call to suffering and separation is a brightness, a wholeness, a loveliness that has never changed from the moment our Creator conceived us, the only intent being Love, Union, Joy, unremitting Happiness.

This we must embrace, this we must fall into, this we must enliven because it is us.

Many of us are still suffering in small and bigger ways, and of course, this is doing its great work of breaking down the cement walls of the self-construct. Breaking us open in vulnerability to love, allowing us to fall gradually into the heart of God.

And there comes a point where the whole charade of the ego must be seen from a higher vantage point. That suffering is just hanging on to a very familiar, darkened room in the house of life. We are reluctant to leave, so very scared. Who's going to hold our hand and protect us from the unknown? But your sweet, sweet hand is already held—something greater and brighter and perfectly safe, enticing you forth into your glorious inheritance. And I say "glorious" with all the sincerity and knowing of this writing hand and heart. What we are is glorious, brilliant, shining, perfect peace.

Dear Parsley, I Love You

July 9

I took a writing class with my dear friend, Ana Ramana last week, and this piece came forth. A sweet childhood memory viewed now from a more expanded place.

Dear Parsley, I Love You

Packing up my lunch for Ana's workshop this morning, already feeling the miracle of it all. How many years since I prepared a sandwich to take forth with me into a day out. Out of the house of sickness and into a heart house of loved ones, of joining, connection, of love and goodwill brimming over.

As so often happens, the parsley does it. I love its perkiness, its greenness. As I pop a little bit in my mouth, tears arise and streams of my young days pop in tenderly and brightly.

It's Friday in Catholic Ireland. Fish for the midday meal. It's near time for Mammy's call to pick some parsley from Guard McCann's garden across the road. Parsley for the white sauce that always accompanied the white, white, soft, flaky fish—ah yes, whiting it was called.

I bounce across the road. Sun shining and oh, how I love Guard McCann's garden and an excuse to enter into its savoriness. Bramble bushes of gooseberries, blackberries, raspberries. I didn't even need to taste them—all the delight just in the seeing.

My little legs find the parsley patch in no time—they know the route well—and oh, the sun is still shining and the light and the garden greens and the warmth on my skin—this must be Heaven.

Very happily I return to Mammy clutching my prize. I know she will say, "Good girl, Margaret." Praise so sparsely measured in my home and culture, I feed on her words. A little heart bursting with pride—as hearts are born and meant to do—brightness overflowing.

What I didn't know then and know now, was how brightly Mammy's heart was shining too, and as the scattered family came home to feast, how each one's shining added to the Light that was my home, extending to my Garden of Eden across the road—into the future of this bright child with many sorrows awaiting, but always lighting the Way into the incredible brightness of True Home.

Be the Light

July 24

Recently, there being a lot of challenge and intensity in the body, I reached out to the Holy Spirit asking: How can we suffer so when we are so Light? How can there be such misery in the body?

A series of thoughts came in immediately. I couldn't doubt the source because I could feel the vibrant and authoritative truth of them.

Be the Light. Be the Light. It's no good knowing you are the Light, you are the Self. It's not enough at all.

You must LIVE it. Be it. Have it. Claim it. Let it course through you. You must rise up in it. As it. Only it.

Make a commitment to this. Go for it. Let everything else that you have clung to for dear life take its rightful place in the mirage that it is.

Walk as it. Talk as it. Greet everyone as it. Don't let anything intrude on This.

Practice. Practice. Practice makes perfection—the Perfection you already are but don't own.

I could feel the great rightness of this and how everything just slides away as we stand as the Truth. Entertaining my physical symptoms is so not being the Light.

Holding and receiving the suffering one takes us as far as it can. When this has become a practice and a gentle eye can greet the experiences of the character, we have met a lot of the self-hatred that runs the show. Now we are ready and ripe to take in the UNREALITY of the show. There is another step to take, that infamous no-step that is right HERE.

We are here "to walk the world a little while." (*A Course in Miracles*) Let not our walking be in vain. Let every step be used to remember only the Truth. There is no walking. There is no earth. There is no world. Only the Light of God—this great Light that blinds out all illusions—the one true, constant, everlasting eclipse.

And with this truth in our hearts, we are free again to walk the world, to love, to bless, to heal, to smile, to join, to laugh, to hug… to play… to play… to play in the now magical, enchanting fields of the Lord.

The End is Certain

July 31

Any inclination to hold on to specialness in any form keeps you from your God-given happiness. Recently I noticed a sneaky little thought of pride, that a certain person would read something I wrote and would think the better of me.

Oh, how foolish is this mind. How lonely it is. How desperate it is, rummaging around its world looking for some scraps of sustenance.

And how tenderly and understandingly I can receive it now. Years of trying to placate it, leading nowhere. Lifetimes of believing it, leading only to suffering. How happily I hand these silly thoughts over now to my Holy, Holy Self. Together, we smile on them noting their unreality, tenderly tucking them away, watching them disappear into soft clouds of oblivion.

Need I say it wasn't always as light and airy as this? Nor is it so all the time. What reams of unworthiness and specialness and hatred must be unearthed before we can lightly look on thoughts and be passers-by! Two scenes of old spring to mind.

Sitting on a bus leaving the holy mountain of Arunachala in Southern India and stating to a friend, "I'm just going to sit here and hate freely!" Three weeks of fervent devotion and attempted silence leading to THIS! What I now understand so well is that it was the very purity of the Mountain that allowed into consciousness and expression this long buried self-hatred that was being projected onto others. The only way out. Alleluia.

Another moment, remembering how my daughter laughed and laughed (knowing my penchant for the dramatic) when I related to her that I had posted on Facebook something about "sitting in the bowels of unworthiness this morning." Oh, the places we must meet and be with as we travel Home.

Our destination is inevitable. It will not seem like that in many, many moments and spells, but yes, it is. We go Home. We ARE Home. Home is what we are.

"We have begun the journey. Long ago the end was written in the stars and set into the Heavens with a shining Ray that held it safe within eternity and through all time as well. And holds it still, unchanged, unchanging and unchangeable."

~ A Course in Miracles

Bringing In the Sunshine

August 7

Some time back I was sitting in the waiting-room of my physical therapist's office and was graced with some true seeing.

Initially, it was as if my perception darkened, and all I could see was the horror of life in separated form. An array of misshapen, scrambled, limping, wheeling-around bodies. All I could think was how could the beauty and perfection of God be reduced to this: half-attempts at some weird life?

I am horrified and moved to tears at the plight of us all. Truly, to not see past the body's appearance is the most depressing thing. I pray to see things differently, to look past what I see with the body's eyes, and I invite in other eyes. Christ vision is one name for it.

The truth of what our brothers are cannot be perceived through the body's eyes. The sensing of light and loveliness is only available to something looking out from the same loveliness. I focus on looking beyond, steadily and surely.

The waiting room is transformed for a short spell as I now see the beauty and perfection of God. What appeared to be so lacking—perfection and light—the way to it seems only enhanced by the magnitude of such contrast. I bless my brothers who are one with me. I thank them for this upliftment into true vision. I want to hug everyone and talk about what a wonderful day it is and how lucky we are to be who we are, but I return quietly to my own world, sensing that my elevation of spirit helps at a level not known and yet known to me. One mind shining reaches, stretches automatically and without effort into other minds because we are one.

"You are wholly lovely. A perfect shaft of pure light."

~ *A Course in Miracles*

Revisiting Self-Compassion

September 19

This remarkable journey inward to the Light: how it weaves around, revisiting at spells wounds you thought were long loved undone. It may seem at times to follow an indirect course, but the absolute rightness of all experience and arisings is revealed as we consciously move through them.

Recently, the need for more compassion and love for my own self made itself very known through another bout of physical debilitation and limited mobility. Waves of vulnerability and the consequent heart opening that accompanies these states were welcomed in graciously but oh, I was acutely disappointed and nearly despairing at the tenacious egoic pattern of feeling some kind of appeasement when hearing of another's life challenge. It felt like it was way overdue for this to be complete, with all the prior work on it and all the heart opening that was being made manifest. Not so. In fact, its painful starkness was even more visceral in contrast to the beauty of what was unfolding.

In sharing with a dear friend and mentor, she said something to me that I believe she has said a hundred times before. "Could you just love this suffering being that is having these thoughts?"

There is a readiness, a ripeness to really hear now, born of the weariness of carrying this pain of separation. I took her advice to heart and every time I noticed any gladness or "misery loves company" when hearing, for example, of someone's fatigue, I paused, just to stop and look. Where is this thought coming from? Straight from an unhappy being. And what did she need right now? The greatest of understanding and love. I could feel my heart opening in gentleness to this misunderstood part of myself. So often still she had been met with judgment and harshness for such "spiritually immature" thoughts.

I found myself saying over and over again, *"You can have whatever thoughts you need to, and I am just here loving you."*

There has been much softening around this in recent weeks, more self-judgment falling away. So simple. And yet the way appears so complicated for so long until the heart is fully primed to love it all.

In summation, a beautiful quote from my spiritual teacher, Devaji:

"You begin to realize that nothing is more important in your life than being there for yourself, the part of yourself that has never experienced being fully received. To completely love yourself, the part of yourself that doesn't know what it's like to be completely loved. It is Love that is your nature that completes the ego so that it is ready to dissolve back into from where it came."

If You Were Me...

September 23

Lying in bed last night, a lot of uncomfortable sensations and contraction in the body. I was having difficulty in receiving just what was there. Wanting to pick up my phone, a guaranteed distraction.

Asking for help to be steady in the allowing, a faint murmuring of thought from the Holy Spirit came in... "If you were Me..."

I didn't need another word. A clear shift in consciousness from toying with what was appearing in the foreground back to the sense of the Vertical. What is steady and quiet and totally unperturbed by the ego's claim to noise and meaning and significance. This vertical backbone that knows the meaninglessness of all form, of all movement, of all mental and physical disturbance.

Sometimes, it's this simple. If you were Me…

Gentleness with the Character

October 3

Gentleness turns the ego on its backside. In a few, precious moments of patience and understanding, it becomes null and void because it survives through judgment and divisiveness, with yourself, with anything.

Many of us are still dealing with addictive-type behaviors and compulsions that we may long to purify and be done with. One morning recently, wide awake at 6 AM, I realize I'm heading for my computer to watch an episode of the TV show, "This Is Us." The mind goes, *Oh no, you're not really going to do that at this time.* Oh yes, she is. She doesn't want to hear anything about an early morning meditation; she wants to luxuriate in some distraction and entertainment.

We're smoking, drinking, eating the "wrong" foods, shopping, internetting—anything at all that we have an argument with—this is where our work continues. And it calls for the utmost gentleness. And to our surprise it can end up being the sweetest feeling of all. A great place to start is to simply place your hand on your heart and address whatever is moving the character in this way. "It's OK, sweetheart. It is so OK. I love you. I am here with you. You can do whatever you need to do right now."

A softness comes in, the recognition that some woundedness is being received, a child-self not held enough is welcomed at last.

Wouldn't we all like to have a "pure" life, that feeling of all in order, of always doing the right thing? Over and over again, we see that it is this very lack of perfection that takes us into the arms of the Beloved. We give up this tight-fisted, limited sense of what's right for the true perfection, ease and gentleness of Love. Where Love is, there is our purity.

Nurturing the Light That You Are

October 9

Back in 2015 I had surgery for a double mastectomy. Some of my spiritual companions tuned into me during the operation and told me later that they saw, felt me as Light. There is no ego in stating this. It is simply a fact. What we all are.

This report seemed to open a new channel for me and a new reign of consciously nurturing the Light. Self-reminding at its highest.

How can we do this?

Tell yourself you are the Light. The Light of God. Over and over, speak the truth to yourself. The Light is in there, in you. It is you. Everything else is make believe. Sense Light in you. Imagine a ray of Light coming out of your chest. Let the sense of body fall away for a bit and let the image of light, the feeling of Light, appear to you in whatever way it will for you. Perhaps you're a nice, soft fuzz ball of Light or something more shiny or piercing. The main thing is to go past the form.

And you will naturally start seeing your dream, the play of your life, with a new eye for noticing your true reflection as

Light mirrored there. It's out there everywhere. A new day dawns; the sun is shining. What is this but the reflection of this Light in you? The sun rippling, dancing on water: what a perfect image for Truth reminding. Bright photos, images that uplift, you're already sensing and being impacted by these. Recognize this even more. Affirming the Truth.

Stop being fooled by form. Start zoning in on the Truth of everyone you meet. They are the Light of God. You are either perceiving flesh or recognizing spirit. Which will you have it be, which one strengthens the knowledge of Truth in you?

"As you see him, so shall you see yourself." ~ *A Course in Miracles*

Beautiful ideas to play with. And I assure you they will stand you in good stead. Focusing on Light is focusing on the presence, the power of God in you. A new sense of Self appears gradually, and you start to feel more expanded, lit up, joyful, happy. You begin to live in the joy of the Self, and you're happy to shine this light wherever you go.

The light of your Creator, your Father. One uninterrupted stream of pure Light.

We But Dream a Dream

November 10

It is kind of shocking to become more and more aware of how we use everything in this dream to deny our divinity. To deny our beauty, our Light, the great Love that we are.

Everything that disturbs us, everything that enthralls us: they are equally mesmerizing and seduce us into the illusion of time and space, of bodies and personalities and matter.

We are a little crazy, wouldn't you say? Deranged. How we deny our supreme happiness for crumbs of specialness and headiness, for pain and suffering and self-punishment in the vain and hopeless pursuit of mitigating the so-called "sin" of deserting our Creator. That never happened at all.

We have no choice now but to keep pulling back out of the dream. Reminding ourselves as frequently as we can that we are indeed dreaming. It's all made up. It has no substance. It's all as flimsy as cobwebs we wipe away with a small thrust of hand.

Let today be a day for remembering. To stand back, to look around wherever you are and remind yourself that you are dreaming. *Ah yes, I made this up. It's all happening in my mind.* Hallucination, imagination, illusion.

And what remains, remains eternally. Even if you can't feel it in this moment, it is You. Supreme happiness, the Light that knows no dimming, the Heart of God.

As we continue to deny the apparent reality of the dream, it will make itself felt. Guaranteed by God.

Equality of All Being

November 17

We hold on to all our *better thans* and *less thans* for dear life. Life as an ego, life with a personal, special identity.

There are ones we elevate, and ones we demote. The ones we raise up in our minds, we don't feel entirely comfortable with them because we're trying to maintain an image; they must like us. The ones we demote: if they seem to be stepping above the station we've assigned them, we're annoyed. I'm remembering an expression from my childhood: "the nerve of them."

We are here to learn how totally and completely equal we are to all beings. Not one shred of difference can ever mar this pristine and pure equality, or we have thrown ourselves out of Heaven—again. Heaven IS equality. Heaven IS sameness.

Our roles on earth appear to be different, appear to have greater or lesser stature, but the truth of our being that shines eternally knows no divisiveness. The energetics of our worldly conditioning, the energetics of a fundamental belief in separation, will continue to seep out and release itself from our bodies and minds. Let us, as best we can, not make a big deal out of this. It's the healing way of it. But this too, these emotions and sensations are not real even as they feel deadly real.

The Light that we all inhabit has one same brilliance. And we can offer back to this Light all crazy notions of fragmentation and specialness. It waits but for this—our willingness. The Light cannot heal what is not given to it. We bring our exposed bellies of darkness and misunderstanding to the greatness that we are, and we give thanks, we never cease to give thanks that our way out, our way back is so clear and so guided by a wisdom beyond us.

Equality of all being—let us rest in and receive the miracle of this today.

Waking Up the Christ in You

December 1

It's the month of Christmas. And I have an invitation for you, for me, for anyone to whom this appeals.

For each day until December 25th, remember to see the Light, to see the Christ in one person. Just one. Someone, anyone. A family member as they come down the stairs, the UPS delivery person, someone you pass on the street, someone you're thinking of. The Light you are is not fussy. It sees Light in everyone.

An invitation to see past appearance, past body, matter, form, to the Truth. Looking beyond what we made up to totally fool ourselves about who we are.

It only takes a few moments, and to help with the focus you can say quietly inside, "My Light blesses you; your Light blesses me." To see the Light in your brother is to see the Light that shines within you. It establishes your true identity and theirs.

And truth is, there are no others out there. Only images projected out from our mind onto the screen of "our life," representing our grievances, judgments and beliefs, or reflecting the beauty of the Self. I saw this on an ayahuasca journey one time and knew it to be the irrefutable truth.

Sensing the Light in another is a simple and powerful practice. And perhaps by Christmas Day, it will have become a new, rich and enlightening habit.

Shall we do this together? I'll be back during the month with some posts to keep us on track.

With love and warm hugs and light, Pema

"The name of Jesus is the name of one who was a man but saw the face of Christ in all his brothers and remembered God."

~ A Course in Miracles

A Namaste of Light

December 8

Continuing our Christ vision assignment…

The most wonderful thing about this practice of sensing another as Light is how it shifts our identification as a body to the exciting Truth of what we are: Light. It is the practice of Self-reminding, Light-reminding, Eternity-reminding.

You are not just coming together as body to body, but as Light to Light, as forever presence to forever presence. A namaste of Light. Start sensing others as Light, even if only for a moment or two, and I promise you Light will start peeking out at you from all aspects of your life.

"… to see the Light in your brother is to see the Light that shines within you, only this. You cannot take this journey without your brother because your brother is you—an expression of yourself. And how you choose to see him, is how you choose to see and experience yourself."

~ Jesus: A New Covenant **

Angels of Light

December 15

Have you seen anyone today that looks like an Angel of Light? The reality is that everyone you've seen or thought of looks like this—well, minus the wings :)

Just to sense a hint of this Light is plenty, plenty. You are forging a new habit and stepping out of the mass hypnosis of believing that the body is what we are. And this is synonymous with stepping out of suffering because the ego uses the body to prove that separation is real.

Let's stop being fooled by form and appearance, and let's zone in on the truth that everyone is an Angel of Light. Let's stop pussy-footing around between what we KNOW to be true and this other sorry state of clinging to smallness and body identification out of conditioned notions of safety and familiarity.

Christmas serves as a reminder that the Light has come, that the Christ is here. And we are Christmas, we are the Christ, we can't not be what we are.

Here now. Truth now. Angels of Light.

Happy Christ

December 25

A happily growing Christ vision to all you dear Christs in my life.

2020

My Holiness Blesses You

January 6

It is our own blessing we are waiting for. Lifetimes of waiting.

It seems we're waiting to make whatever body/character we're "enshrined" in palatable to this other part of the mind, the spiritual ego. Which it never will be. It's designed that way, the whole ego and world having erupted out of the energy of self-hatred. So, it's a lost cause that a program of self-hatred can do anything other than reject. Computer programs don't buck half-way through a run and decide to do something different.

We can never expect this program of self-judgment to be different. It will find its favorite causes for reproach, always.

It's our own true blessing we wait for, from outside the program of self-condemnation. We can interrupt and arrest a cycle of self-dislike with this Self-blessing: *My Holiness blesses you.*

Practice it a little, a lot. Repeat the words, letting the grace come in.

My Holiness blesses you—sweet, guilt-laden, fictional creature that you are.

My Holiness blesses you—and sees no wrong. It cannot see error because "you" are not real.

My Holiness blesses you—and understands the enormous suffering you have inflicted on yourself through this parody of judgment and attempted self-correction.

My Holiness blesses you—and declares your eternal innocence.

My Holiness blesses you—and watches as once again you recede into that soft background of invisibility.

My Holiness blesses you—and only my sweet Holiness remains.

Breast Surgery and Truth

January 10

My dear daughter, Orna, had a mastectomy this week for breast cancer. Living in different time zones I was wide awake at 4.30 am, her appointed surgery time. I wanted to join with her, to be with her, to support her in any which way I could from a distance.

As I settled into feeling into her, there were images of what was going on. A young woman's breast. A surgeon's knife. Absolutely perfect fodder for a mind to go to tragedy and what "shouldn't" be happening. And I expected my mind to pick this up and run with it, to feel the emotions of sadness and despair at this young, beautiful body being mutilated. In a weird way I was nearly pushing the mind in this direction out of some distorted sense that this must be felt.

To my surprise, the mind couldn't go there. Instead, there was this steady sense of who my daughter really was as Light. A feeling of complete invulnerability in her to what was happening to her body. I remained in this expanded state for quite some time. A steadfastness of ease and lightness, of being way above the battleground. Of there being no battleground.

I could also sense how she had signed up for this, that all was well, that she was in the safest hands of all—God's hands. In the hands of Life that knew her course and could guide her safely and lovingly. So far beyond what I as simply her biological mother could ever do.

It all felt like grace, but I also "knew" that it was a grace born of a consistent practice this past year of looking out at other beings through my spiritual eyes—as often as I could remember—to see past body appearance to the pure Light that every form attempts to hide and deny.

Giving thanks right now for the grace of our lives where transformation is a daily, weekly experience. Our perfectly guided curriculum that walks us all into that Light and Love where tragedy has no meaning because form has no meaning. That infinite Light of Being where nothing sticks—the Light that "can remove all pain, can end all sorrow, and can solve all problems." Let us hasten our way there.

Marinate as Light

January 19

You are Light. The rest of it, as in everything else, is foreign. It looks so familiar, the everyday routine, your home, your loved ones—how can all this possibly be foreign?

I'm telling you it is. It's just habit, familiar images in the mind, forms that seem so dense and real. That's what hallucination is—that's what it looks like—your everyday world.

Trump is happening in your mind. Iran is happening in your mind. Presidential elections are happening in your mind. Your kitchen, your living-room, your workplace is happening in your mind. All the thousands of thoughts about how you as a small self are doing, are all in your mind. You as a small self, as a body, is in your mind.

It's all mind. And now what do we do?

You recognize this, and you give the whole kit and kaboodle back to your Father. All it brings is misery, the misery of separation. You may cry for a bit at the craziness of it all, the perceived stuckness, hopelessness or whatever the particular baseline of your construct is.

And then you focus on what you are: Light. You contemplate

Light. You marinate as Light. I like to imagine the heavens opening up above me and beaming Light down on me. Let any images of Light that come to mind come in. This is your real home, as the umpteen near death experiences you've read about proclaim. And you know it. You wouldn't be reading this if you didn't know it.

It doesn't matter what's happening with the body; it's your so-called home for such a short time. Stay as the Light. You have to be determined. The pull of mind is so strong.

Stay and let the Light work its magic on you for a while. Obliterating the world. Calming the heart. Stilling everything. Resting in God. Resting at home. Resting as Light.

Leaving the Sandbox of Dreams

February 24

It's time to stop playing in the sandbox. It's time to stop blaming the other child for throwing sand at you. It is sooo time to put "unfairly treated" and "victim" aside and recognize the nature of this dream.

We set it up to make it look like someone/something is doing something to us when all the time, deep in the cloisters of our unconscious mind, we set it up to be exactly as it is playing for us.

"I have invented the world I see." ~ *A Course in Miracles*

You might ask why in the name of goodness would we ever set this up this way. Nobody wants to experience upset and pain. But we made up this whole cosmos as a hiding place, a playing field for the ego. We so didn't want to feel the enormous, unconscious guilt we carry from breaking away from our Creator. We tried to lighten the load of our pain by getting lost in this kaleidoscope of color and movement and distraction and most importantly, projection.

We would project the dark contents of our mind onto others and situations that seem EXTERNAL to us. They are guilty; we are innocent. The surviving cry of the ego, "it's their fault." The untold power and relief of projection which is no relief at all because guilt is the greatest cling-on and cannot leave its source, the mind of the projector.

But in this world of time and space there is one wonderful thing we can do when we find ourselves blaming another. We can forgive. Truly forgive. We can reel back our projections and with a joyful heart hand them over to Spirit, who waits with infinite patience and infinite love to help us release every scrap of ego belief, emotion and perception.

Unraveling it all, returning to Light and Love. Recognizing the wellspring of goodness that has always resided in our hearts. What a meaningful, worthwhile way to live that promises eternal happiness.

(For a practical application of forgiveness, see the Steps to Forgiveness on page 256.)

Give No Truth to the Dream

March 3

I am not going to know true happiness until I have stepped all the way out of this dream. As long as I am pulled back in for anything, I am bound. Bound to an illusion that doesn't work. Can never work because it was built on separation.

Just to look around at this world. You see separation and fragmentation everywhere. All of us in different bodies, little fenced-off areas that we call ourselves. Conflict of some sort with others if not constantly, then regularly. A separated mind doesn't know peace because peace only comes from union and unified perception.

Knowing we are One, no one to be better than or less than, no one to have more than or less than. No color or race or status that can differentiate. In Oneness, we are seeing past all of these disguises, masks, personas to the Light that everyone is. We don't even say "inhabit" because we can't inhabit Light. We ARE Light. And then we pretend to wear a costume to deny our divine reality. It's called madness.

Give no truth to the dream. See it for what it is. A dark experience in hallucination of the greatest order. A cosmos of wispiness to which we attempt to give the status of reality.

We have been fooled. We have fooled ourselves big time. But the Light of Truth shines eternally, inviting us, appealing to our right minds, awaking that same Light in us that can penetrate and make mincemeat out of any illusion.

My prayer this morning: that I may know the Truth with all of my heart and return to the supreme happiness I am.

Tenderness Being Born

April 5

When we are butted up against the unresolvable over and over again, there is a tenderness that eventually springs forth as if from the Heart of God Himself.

This tenderness wraps its arms around all of it, the situation and all that it evokes in the body and mind. All of it crumbles into this even expanse of gentleness and love.

Seamless. Without seams. Not even a tiny wrinkle between

the love in your heart and what was once perceived as so challenging. Tender tears flow. Hard-wrung out of us but now worth every moment of distress as they wet and soften and bless the landscape of our minds.

What you thought was a hard crust of earth that must disappear for peace to be yours, you now see that in its watering and loving, it has every right to be. And you could stroke it forever.

Thank you, dear unresolvable dream, for breaking down this small will with its silly, innocent and decided ideas about how things should be and where happiness lies.

And we continue on our way with a softer and more surrendered heart, on our way to seeing the whole world through the blessed eyes of our very own holiness.

Raising the Bar: Body Identification

April 13

Losing investment in how the body is doing or feeling is a huge process. After many years of sickness, I can safely say it takes the time it takes.

Being unconcerned with the body's welfare goes hand in hand with recognizing yourself as spirit. You can't hold onto both. It's a no-brainer. You're one or the other. However, the attachment to the body as who we are is huge. It's not even that we look at our body and proclaim it as ourselves. It is so much more embedded than that. We've been steeped in, fully submerged in body identification since the day we were born. An assumption that is never questioned until you get on a serious spiritual way or the body starts falling apart—its bright and certain destiny:)

Let us raise the bar today on where we want our allegiance to be. Flesh that will sicken, die and decay or invulnerable Light that shines forever.

When sickness of any nature appears, every mind instinctively wants correction. We want to patch it up, get our wee kingdom back on track. It's natural and normal and just plain kindness to want to relieve suffering. But sometimes nothing seems to work, and this is where Truth can step in more fully and use the situation for its one and only purpose—to push us, grow us, Truth us out of body identification.

With every rumble of trouble, can we use it in the deepest way? To remind ourselves it is not real, it is not everlasting, neither the rumble nor the body. Can we turn towards the Light as our default mechanism? Can we do some serious raising of the bar instead of the endless twirling of mind around cause and diagnosis and what it means? (This is not to say that infinite patience may be called for with these mechanisms of mind and the fear that's engendered around body distress.)

Let all body dysfunction be a call to the Light that's always shining down on you and out from you. A call to Heaven's always open door and a receiving of what you have always been. The Light is here, and the way is clear.

One Hundred Percent Responsibility

April 19

When I get triggered recently, I love to remind myself that I am 100% responsible for my sight, for my perception and projection—they are one thing.

Something about saying I'm 100% responsible a few times

to myself just helps flip my mind back from the story I'm spinning. Cuts off the external presentation.

There was a time in our relationships when we felt magnanimous and wise when we could say that any relationship had a 50-50 responsibility dynamic. But that time is long over.

Your world is your thoughts embodied out there in people and movement and circumstances. It's all yours. Which is the great, good news because now you can affect how you feel about it. If you weren't the dreamer of your dream, something else would rule over you, and you would be a victim indeed.

To affect change in our perception, all that is needed is our willingness. Our willingness to not like or want how we feel in this separation mode. To WANT unity and oneness again. Your Holy Self does all the work once our willingness is in place. It's not your job to try and force your heart open or to feel love for someone you're projecting onto. Not your responsibility.

It all becomes so much easier and more effective when you realize that's the Holy Spirit's function. You give Him everything that would hurt you, acknowledging your mind is 100% responsible for what you're feeling and thinking. Then you sit back and let Love flow in sometime later and surprise you with its simplicity.

Every character has a favorite array of knots and stories and issues, and they come back around over and over again. Don't be surprised at this. Each time, they may hurt a little less or not. The main thing is that the layers of separation-guilt are dissolving and at some point, your favorite trip-up won't touch you anymore.

How blessed we are to have a way out of the darkness of separation. How miraculous is our Teacher and Friend, our own Self that knows how to unravel every single loop of mind into the Light and Love that never ceased to shine or care. We just missed it for a while.

A Day of Innocence

April 27

Imagine dedicating a full day to freedom from thoughts of guilt or wrongdoing of any nature. How sweet, peaceful and restful this could be.

Twinges of wrongdoing can lie at the base of many of our activities and thinking ways. We rarely get to feel totally innocent and carefree. But innocence is our nature, so how can we begin to match our days with our Nature?

Often, often we are doing something, and the mind is saying we should be doing something else… or whatever we're doing, we're not doing it quite right. We're goofing off when we could be meditating. We're eating when we're not hungry, or we're not following some lovely diet idea for health and image. We're social media-ing too much or watching too many shows.

We're not having nice, pure, loving thoughts, or we're not meeting whatever darkness is showing up with enough awareness.

It's endless at times, how that mind can bully us into a knot of wrong or off. And that's its job. This is how it maintains the guilt of separation. The last thing in the world that the ego wants you to do is to feel guiltless and to feel loving and loved. As long as we're feeling bad about something, anything, the ego reigns. And we just continue to replay that mad, mad moment where we believed ourselves separate and felt consumed with wrongness.

For just one day—today—we can bring a ton of consciousness to this program. Let's be innocent and free, children again, playing in the world of whatever we're doing.

Walk in the sunshine of "no guilt." Eat in the sunshine of "no guilt." Play, do, don't do in the sunshine of "no guilt."

It's just another way of letting Light and Love bless our very existence, which it is doing ALL THE TIME anyways. It knows nothing of wrongdoing. Couldn't see it if it had neon lights flashing all around it. Only the benevolence, purity and loveliness of Self.

Amen to that and amen to our true way of being in the day, moving freely, simply doing what we're doing, innocent and carefree. It's just a dream after all.

Becoming God's Open Book

May 7

We keep some of our thoughts private because we are ashamed of them: They're not holy enough, or they point to a persona we do not want to be. You would hide yourself from God because you believe somehow you are bad. But hiding brings no healing, only continued misery.

It's a beautiful thing to decide you don't want to do this anymore. The honesty of God is calling us.

What is it about holding on to private thoughts that would keep us from our freedom? In themselves, they actually mean nothing. They are all illusionary as only the loving thoughts of God have any reality. In our reluctance to share them, in our judgment of them, we are making them real in our minds. In hiding them, we maintain this closed off section of the mind that is not available for a full healing.

Offering all of ourselves to our brothers and sisters takes courage but the relief and radiance it brings is the proof of the pudding. You are letting Light into previously darkened pockets.

Being transparent is not about spewing all the contents of your mind out all over the place. It's a measured discernment, noticing where you're feeling some hesitation to share thoughts with a friend, a loved one. It's a checking in and asking for guidance as to what is appropriate and what is healing and in steadfast courage offering your mind back to your Holy Self through sharing with others.

Many thoughts are brought to our Holy Self regularly as an inside job. Sometimes where there is a lot of stickiness, shame, guilt, you bring them to the Light of God through the intermediary of another. A safe "other" becomes the Holy Spirit for you.

Utter transparency is joyous; it's childlike, it's freedom, it's carefree. Let us not delay in giving total goodness to ourselves. Turn toward the Light and it will sweep out all imagined darkness forever.

Life on Hold—Never

May 20

Connecting with my daughter this morning on WhatsApp and we're interrupted with the images of each other disappearing and "call on hold" showing up on the screen.

Call on hold. Life on hold. I don't think so. Tears visit my eyes for the richness of it all. Another precious opportunity to remember what's real.

Images come and go, their one purpose being their nothingness. They are totally united in that one sweeping wave of meaninglessness. We can wipe them all away. There is no hierarchy in illusion, one image or happening having no more substance or weight or meaning than another. Illusion is illusion is illusion.

My daughter has disappeared from sight, but now I see her even more truly as I take these moments to tune into what in her can never disappear. The sense of Light, her God-given perfection and wholeness. Her self as God created it, unchanging, eternal, glowy beingness. And this all being translated unknowingly by my mind as "me too." This is what I am.

We are visited by many calls on hold in our day, literally and metaphorically. Let us remember to use them wisely. Always being given second and third and an everlasting array of chances to gladden and brighten our hearts in the glow of Truth.

To bless ourselves as we bless the other. To namaste, to bow down, to be lifted up together. I bless you, I honor you, I love you. Are there any sweeter words than these? Any sweeter feeling? Not in my book of life, so far.

Letting the Love In

July 10

Let the Love in, sweetheart. Let this merciful Love put its arms around you, in whatever sorry condition you find yourself.

How eager it is to bless you and hold you and stroke you, everything that it knows so well to do that is soothing and completing for you. Filling in any gaps of prior unlovedness.

It is in the air, all around you. Your whole life, it has been around you, waiting, waiting, the most patient lover you could ever have. A lover that doesn't even know what patience is, not in its realm of existence nor in its vernacular. Just THERE.

We cannot feel it until we do. The walls of mind take their own time in crumbling. The dark nights, the slow burns, the self-hatred that seems to encase you and feels like cement at times. What can we do but do our work and give everything that hurts back to this great love? Over and over and over again.

And in the grace-filled moments that we feel its presence and beneficence, let us remember this is what we are—this softness, this tenderness we are floating in all the time.

We invite it in even closer, all the way to the marrow of our bones, stroking the limbs of the unloved child until the sweetness outside touches the sweetness inside, the last piece of the jigsaw puzzle gently laid in place, the picture complete.

Only this Love.

Empty Hands

July 21

Specialness is the ego's substitute for God's love. Specialness and individuality are the same; neither one can ever bring happiness, the happiness that springs from Truth, the happiness that is naturally happy without cause or thinking about why it's happy. A fountain that doesn't question where the water comes from.

Specialness is quite different. It has a mental reason to feel good, to feel slightly pumped up over something or other, some place it has excelled, it has "beaten" your brother in the comparison race, and it likes the feeling of superiority. Finally, you have some importance and acknowledgment. It doesn't last, of course, because in the next breath there is a thought of someone "beating" you. In our younger spiritual days, the feeling of specialness would have satisfied us quite well, making up for the story of unworthiness we carried so vigilantly.

But specialness no longer satisfies. It offers only the opposite now because it smacks of separation and divisiveness. And you, beautiful you, are no stranger now to the ways of the Heart, the inclusiveness, the God tears, the gratitude for the bigness of who you eternally are. The jarring note of specialness cannot hold a candle to the tenderness and aliveness of the open heart.

How happy are we now to have a way to bring our false, carved-out-of-separation, self-concept Home? We but need to notice these specialness thoughts; we need not even frown over them as their unreality is more deeply known. We offer them back to our Holy Self in the firm certainty that they are being absolved and taken care of.

Our prayer to come all the way home has become more ardent; our desire to have only the loving thoughts of God fill our minds has become the most important thing. And we come now to our Father, empty for a moment of "me," empty of our usual distractions, empty of hope in a hopeless dream.

"Hold onto nothing. Do not bring with you one thought the past has taught, nor one belief you ever learned before from anything. Forget this world, forget this course, and come with wholly empty hands unto your God."

- A Course in Miracles

Walking in My Own Divinity

July 27

In this strange limbo of existence that I experience these times with serious illness, not knowing the fate of this body in terms of staying or leaving, I have many visitations of physical weakness and frailty. It can be so automatic to succumb to the predominant feelings of feebleness and have that take over my consciousness.

Over time, however, this very experience of body weakness has been holding out its hand, generously offering me my true strength. Weakness in the body becomes a call for love, a call for going vertical, a call for right seeing. I've come to naming it 'Walking in my own Divinity." When I can, I focus not on what's wrong with the body but on what is right in spirit and is forever right and unchanging.

Just saying what are for me these powerful words, "Walking in my own Divinity," serves to lift me out of a bad dream that is so not serving me when believed. A new found strength arises that lifts the spirit into what is real and permanent and forever shining. The great ray of Light that I truly am announces its existence in whatever subtle or serious way it does. The extent of the experience makes no difference; it's a shifting of gears, and the master switch has been turned on.

Shifting identity from the fantasied belief in weakness and powerlessness, the domain of the ego, back to my original nature—Truth, that knows the lie and meaninglessness of the body, whether sick or well. Lifting me out of the barriers of time and space and into the experience of lightness with ever more lightness awaiting. The antechamber of Heaven.

The body may or may not respond with more strength. In the moment it feels irrelevant because I am filled with a wholeness that decades of a healthy body never could give me. Tears of strength and recognition and gratitude spring forth as I realize once again there is nothing wrong with my world. There is nothing wrong with my body, just an appearance in a sorry dream of matter and energy but seen through the vision of the sage, it takes on the holiness and the benevolence of the eyes that rest on it.

For those of us challenged with illness and compromised bodies, we can take great heart in the knowing that these circumstances are a mighty catalyst in breaking free from form. Nothing seems to uproot us out of the body more than a sick body. And this uprooting is mandatory if we are to know ourselves truly. No half-way measures; we are either flesh or spirit.

The physical body walks, or it doesn't. But You are always walking, jumping, skipping Home. Walking in Light, in your own enlivened, precious Divinity.

Give the Mind Back to Heaven

September 6

A dear friend came to visit me this week. We go back a long way, and there has been much healing and goodwill in our relationship for some time.

She's recounting to me how she is making progress with her physical health and exercise. It was only later that I noticed the thought of what we call envy or jealousy, that thought of wanting her to be in the same place as me with my body when I am believing my story. Challenged and limited.

Initially, there was a feeling of dismay, that after all my work, these thoughts could still be arising and causing disturbance.

That my serenity and peace are only sustained if "they are not doing better than me, if they are doing worse than me." Such familiar thought patterns for this construct.

But the good news is that I do know the way Home. I know that giving back these separating thoughts to the Beloved is all I have to do. And I can do that in the most lighthearted way. In this case, I could feel the thought being lifted up, airborne, going back to its origin of a kind of nowhere. What a relief to know that I am being brought even closer to my heart's desire, a mind that holds only the loving thoughts of God.

There are a few tears of release that seem to round out the heart, bringing it back to a softer place.

Some of us are rooted enough in the Self that the meaninglessness of all thought, positive or negative, can hold sway. Some of us prefer and need the practice of "giving the mind back to God." Thought by thought, belief by belief. Until the mind is fully aerated, the conditioning of separation is broken up and only goodness prevails. Much, much prior work will have been done on releasing repressed energies and emotions before these practices can become the simple ones they are.

Give the mind back to Heaven. Practice and practice some more. And as you do this, let your dear eyes light up at the goodness you are beginning to see in all your brothers and sisters. What a treasured task you have been given. What a loving and joyous function you have now that will make your days so much happier and more meaningful.

Walk with the bright step of divine purpose, that inner heart smile that extends out to hugs and joining and goodwill and blessing to all.

A World of Heart

September 18

Issues come back around and around. Layers of misunderstanding being peeled off.

It will look so much at times that you are being unfairly treated. Like you have every right to hold a grievance. Like you have the worst karma of all.

This is where an understanding of metaphysics can help you as you remember that your mind set it up this way. The Big Bang could just as easily be called The Big Blame. A cosmos of conflict, appearance of "others" out of oneness. So we could blame our spouses, our parents, our bosses, etc. The painful guilt we carried from believing we left Heaven, we needed to place that somewhere and try to feel innocent. The battle cry of our earthly kingdom became "it's your fault."

And the remedy is: it's not your fault, it's not my fault because we are imagining the whole play.

There is such relief in remembering that there is no world. A vast relief that can open into the experience of our long forgotten real world. A world of heart where brothers come to love, to be, to feel, to smile, to speak of favorable things, of kind things. Where goodness and goodwill are like drops of moisture in the air waiting to be drunk by every heart whose essence now is only that of cherishing.

A world made new.

A world we now remember and claim.

A world of quiet gratitude for the Creator who made us eternally so.

Giving the Darkness Over to the Holy Self

October 14

What is it in our systems that loves to bully us and proclaim how wrong and inadequate we are? What is it that calls for this chronic kind of self-attack? Everyone knows this patterning intimately; all that varies is the nature of the criticism.

Unconscious GUILT is what keeps this machinery of mind going. Plain, old guilt because we believe we did something woefully wrong, as in leaving our Father and wanting to have a special, unique identity. Guilt demands punishment, and so we have no choice but to attack ourselves.

Getting on the bandwagon of trying to improve and fix the character, to make it adequate and holy keeps us nicely stuck and spinning our wheels because the guilt will just erupt in another area. Healing the belief in guilt and wrongdoing is our ticket Home.

Whenever we feel wrong about some behavior or some imagined inadequacy, recognize this is another layer of guilt arising from the unconscious. We can even be glad that it is so, that it is surfacing to be seen and released. Not that this is always easy to be seen quickly as guilt is decidedly uncomfortable and seductive, and it can take a while to orient ourselves as to what is going on.

The healing of guilt and the proclamation of our innocence is not our job. It is the function of our Holy Self who is so happy to take this layer of darkness into the Heart. We just have to give it over to Him.

What grace that our way out of a dream of suffering is getting clearer and clearer. Closer and closer. And all at the same time we are recognizing there is nothing to overcome. Nothing to overcome because there is nothing there in the first place.

Let us end this self-hypnosis and gullibility. God knows, we've tinkered with it long enough. We step outside of imagined linear time and plonk our two feet firmly in the haven and heaven of God's Love. And let us stay there, forever peaceful as we were created to always be.

A Christ Blessing for You at Thanksgiving

November 26

This, or any part of it, is a powerful way to remember another's divinity. Saying it quietly to yourself when with someone, thinking of someone or watching some character, images on TV—you recognize their holiness and yours at the same time. Generally, you will feel the upliftment of truth.

We are always just seeing ourselves. We are but one mind.

Christ Blessing

I bless you. I honor you. I love you.

You are the Light of Heaven. You are the Light of God.

You are totally innocent. No matter what you do, a dream is a dream and cannot touch your eternal, shining Innocence.

You are perfect. You are whole. You are complete.

You are my holy brother.

I bless you. I honor you. I love you. I thank you.

Nothing Has Changed

December 26

Nothing has changed since we were first created as extensions of God's Love and Peace and Goodwill. Nothing has changed. Everything is intact, untouched, undisturbed. And always will be. Even if storms rage around us and about us and over us and underneath, we are the impermeable spaces of God's love.

Light pours out from us even when we are unaware of it. Love pours out from us even if we only feel vestiges of it or conflict is our immediate experience. Goodwill lies inside, dormant but alive. Goodwill that we are secretly pouring onto everyone we meet.

Can we bring our true and secret lives out to the forefront of our experience? Indeed we can.

For moments and spells, we stop seeing with our false, mortal eyes. Imagine that great Light surrounding you and shining out from you. Imagine the unbounded love that rests in the heart and being of the one you're with, regardless of what is being presented.

And as for goodwill, how sweet it is to bless your friend. You bless them with your own, great holiness, obliterating all the crazy attempts at hostility that feel so real but don't have an ounce of reality to call their own. Made-up conflict. Bless your brother instead. "I bless you. I honor you. I love you. I thank you. "

Reaching down into the Truth of you, drawing it forth and piercing through the clouds of ego in both of your minds. Hold onto the Truth. Interrupt your foggy, seductive mind over and over. Create a cocoon of grace, right there between your heart and another's and for a sacred moment, feel it becoming that one heart of inclusion, equality and upliftment.

Nothing has changed. Despite the innumerable times we've run around this earth and universe, lost in linear time, believing in moving bodies and images and phenomena—an imagined world of shadows and separation.

Nestled in the heart and ready to expand with just our own longing and encouragement lies "the greatest story ever told." The only thing that's not a story. The rock of Truth that is our Father's House, our eternal shelter, our one abiding Home.

2021

The Great Prodding

January 5

What a strong tendency there is to believe that if we could change something about ourselves, our circumstances, all would be so much better. That we would move out of "stuckness" and into greater freedom and ease.

What we don't realize is that the "stuckness" is already inside. The energetics of it, the belief in it is here in our unconscious minds, and the present circumstances are just the inevitable outward picturing.

We use up an incredible amount of mental energy in trying to figure out what to do about our situation. We talk about it to others, seeking counsel, a way out. We wallow in it at times, playing the victim habit, and that can even feel weirdly good at moments—at least it's not our fault.

All of these ways are how the ego keeps us stuck even more in our predicament.

And all the while there is a great prodding from Spirit happening. A tremendous prodding from the Beloved saying, "Wake up, sweetheart. Wake up. It's a dream. Who you are has nothing to do with this mess."

"Stuckness" is the green light for the Vertical. Whenever we feel hopelessness, despair, something unresolvable, we must go High. We go High, and we abandon the horizontal with its endless enticements, loops and cul-de-sacs.

High. Vertical. Light. A stand for Truth, a pillar of Truth.

We are perfect as we are. The stodge of the dream has no effect on us. We remember we are perfect Light, and we let that illuminate us and determine how we feel. Uplifted, strong, out of denial of our own incredible holiness. Letting the stagnation of the dream fall back into the recesses of our minds and suddenly just be gone.

A sense of wholeness takes over, a certainty that all is well. What felt so paralyzing a few moments ago has no meaning now at all as the Truth beams into our minds, eclipsing all the imagined phenomena we have played with so diligently.

We are perfect, pure Light—the Home we go to, the Home that will never cease to prod us and do whatever it takes until we make it our one, true, shining Identity.

(The ability to go Vertical and sense the Light is determined a lot by how much purification of mind has already happened, how much of the ego has already been thinned out. In the earlier stages of our spiritual work, heavy conditioned energies are not easy to rise out of and will need to be purged and allowed to run their course. Gradually, everything gets lighter and the ability to rise out of the dream over and over again becomes easier.)

I Light You

January 22

Anything dark in your life that you're trying to push away, be done with, any pattern of mind that you're not too proud of. Bodily pain and discomfort. Any form of separation at all, anything less than the beautiful unity that is all that is real… there are many ways we've learned to deal with them.

One way that has come to me recently is to repeatedly address the object of mind and say, "I Light you. I Light you. I Light you."

It's strange languaging, I know, but it can have a very effective response in your being.

I Light you.

I notice when I say it to a negative pattern of mind, it seems to lift it up a bit, isolate it out from the general heaviness and density of mind. It gives it buoyancy, and then with tears in my eyes, I notice that it seems to break it apart, like sunlight gently and brightly dispersing the clouds.

I am Light. We are all pure, perfect Light, placed in us by God. There is nothing in us that cannot be touched and neutralized and lit up by this Light. Where we have made darkness, we now bring the light of the Heavens to it.

I Light you, each and every one of you. You Light me, and I thank you.

"The Great Light always surrounds you and shines out from you. How can you see the dark companions in a light such as this?"
~ Jesus in *A Course in Miracles*

A Landscape of Kindness

January 29

My prayer of the heart for some time now has been to have only loving and kind thoughts appear in my consciousness. Only the loving thoughts of God. A non-judgmental atmosphere that is our natural inheritance.

With the wearing down of the ego that the Beloved has masterfully taken charge of, the landscape of this mind and spirit has certainly softened in the direction of kindness. And I am very aware of those moments where the old, mechanical ways of separating still look for a foothold. Out of nowhere, perhaps in a conversation with a friend or alone in thought, I notice how the mind wants to think, say, hang onto something negative about somebody. A rising thought with an accompanying unpleasant energetic and yet enticing and seductive.

Sometimes it wins out, and I find myself making that negative remark. And this is alright. But my learning curve is to notice the potential comment arising and to hold steady in not giving in to it. These are ways and thoughts I no longer want to have cloud up and embitter my consciousness. This is all I need to proclaim. I don't want them anymore. And I can gratefully hand these thoughts back to the Holy Spirit where their dissolution is a given.

The rewards are big. A peaceful heart, a landscape of kindness that can extend out and out without meeting one morsel of conflict. The "peace that passeth understanding" is our natural Home and our holy Self is steering us there unerringly. We need but listen and choose again how we would be: the ego's dutiful servant in all things negative, separating and miserable or the benign child of kindness, whose place at the table of goodness is already set. It has always been set, always patiently waiting for its children to come home and partake of the sacred feast.

"Surely goodness and kindness shall follow me all the days of my life; And I shall dwell in the house of the Lord Forever."

~ Psalm 23:6

Let us join together in a life given over to goodness, kindness and innocence—what we undeniably are.

ALLOW

February 2

I love the word ALLOW.

Like a good friend it reaches gently into my resisting mind and reminds me of the Truth. What I am resisting, I am making real. And making anything real or substantial in this world where all is unreal is getting on the fast track to unhappiness, struggle and spinning mind.

Letting the cool and quieting voice of ALLOW enter our troubled waters is the antidote to struggle. Just saying it a few times first brings our attention to what exactly it is we're not allowing. Gives it a little space away from busy, resisting, fearful mind.

Is it some physical pain, distress, some story line of rejection, unworthiness? Whatever it is, try to bring it down to the lowest common denominator of sensation, contraction in the body. Lay down the thoughts as best you can. And we just sit here, lie here, receiving, allowing.

ALLOW is the entrance of spirit, the smoothing of ruffled feathers. Letting it seep in, we are not so cluttered up in the resistance. Things are calmer. Our world is calmer, as it should be.

Mastery and dominion over what we have invented begins with a gentle Allow. We must be with the egoic appearance until it is clear our fear of it is gone. We stop the fight, disrupt the trance, disengage from unreality.

Be defenseless with the pain, the contraction. Make no story of it. Have no attachment to it and see it cannot affect in any way who you really are.

Peace is outside the world of our making. Peace is—prior, during and after our belief in this world and all that appears to appear.

Into the Hygge of the Heart

February 9

Hygge is a Danish word used when acknowledging a feeling or moment as cozy, charming or special.

Clear, clear spaces of upliftment and feelings of being "above the battleground" open for all of us along our path. And dense, heavy energies come to visit regularly too. Clearing out the debris of the soul's choice for separation.

You will be brought to places and points many times that you feel you cannot endure. The most important work of all. When endurance is stretched to a limit, the light and love are so close. The unbearableness of the mind is exactly what cracks it open.

As the Love rushes in, you realize more deeply that anything you're shut down to, anything you want to avoid, anyone you want to pull down a peg or two is you shutting out a part of precious, beautiful you, shoving you out in the cold. Something opens inside, and you find yourself wanting to wrap this "thing" up ever so tenderly, put a bow on it, make sweet, sweet friends with it, stroke it and bring it into the hygge of the heart. Never to be banished again.

And little by little, every vestige of separation and individuality truly does come home into the Heartland.

Gratitude for the Real

February 21

Yesterday, after a few days of more fatigue than usual, I came down the stairs with a little more energy. My mind went pretty quickly to gratitude, thanking my holy Self for the newfound ability.

It is beautiful to feel gratitude. Anything that promotes this is so welcomed. But I also noticed that I was thanking my Self for an illusion. For something transient. Something that may not be here tomorrow.

It is always best to go deeper with our thankfulness. To honor what is real. What is lasting. What is eternal.

And so, we are grateful for who we are, what we are: Love, Light, children of God. What can never be taken from us, or tampered with or destroyed. What will always be here tomorrow, as long as linear time appears.

Our Eternal Self.

In our gratitude for this, in our focus on it, we are training the mind to remember we are the Light. For a few moments, minutes, we are That again. And "again and again" will bring us seamlessly into the consistent awareness that we are dreaming this dream. And what happiness is this—to look out from the Real, to shine the Light of our holiness on all things, to see the face of God in all. To give up the world we don't want for the world we do want.

The Happy Dream—where we live at last in who we truly are.

The Tenderized Dream

March 12

How gentle and kind your dream appears to be when the heart has become tenderized. Even when the ego mind would normally label the circumstances as challenging, they no longer appear so to You. Something has taken over. Something recognizes the so-called difficulties as your last forays into the mirage of separation and that they are really serving you.

Serving you to finally remove yourself from the whole idea that this world that appears in front of you is separate from you.

With each appearance of separation, you are drawn further into the heart of love, and you are perceiving more and more readily from there.

And how soft and mild and safe it all becomes. How harmless and innocent. With what gratitude and love do you greet your day. Feelings of inclusion for everything, of wanting to pull all things closer to you. Your only function now is to hug and to love what appears.

You bow down and you bow down because you never thought such beauty could be yours. All the years of processing and burning and washing out of the small, mythical me: you are profoundly grateful for all of it, even as it seems to sit in another life.

This Beauty is our fate. Our inheritance. Our incredible God-given inheritance.

Let us make haste Here. Giving this chaotic mind of fragmentation back to Heaven with every opportunity and grace-guided moment we have. Heaven is what we are. A state of mind where perfection reigns and only happiness and goodness see the light of day. The Light of God. Our immortal reality.

The Equality of Truth

April 2

Much healing can happen now in quiet ways of contemplation and reflection. Big purging is not necessarily needed. Ego thoughts are lighter and can be airlifted off of us more easily back into Source.

Recently I was remembering a neighbor of mine from all of thirty years ago. A young woman that my mind had a kind of subtle, permanent positioning of looking down on. I was superior. She was inferior. There were some quick feelings of remorse, regret, sadness that I had not seen her beauty nor appreciated the lovely friendship being offered.

And my mind stretches out and takes in the nature of this construct as a whole. Its competitive, comparative ways of seeing the world and others. Seeking some worth someplace, it looked for my superiority. Being bound by the unconscious guilt of the ego and its natural self-hatred, it could at other times only see my inferiority.

I thank my neighbor for playing this character for me. She is representative of a whole litany of characters and beings in my life. I am now, gratefully, so open to correction. I invite in her true essence. I sense the Light radiating out from her heart, that Light that can never be diminished through thousands of years of silly role-playing.

The mind is again quiet and still and peaceful. I join with her and the Christ mind in this total equality of Truth. How joyous it becomes. Both of us beaming, shining. And everyone I've ever played this game of comparison with comes to join us. Our gratitude is so profound because the contrast between life experienced as this separate entity and life cradled in the bosom of our holy Self is so marked.

How gracious is our Creator. The distributor of love and well-being and unity. This love that is packed into our hearts and can never be emptied out. Our fountain of goodness. Shining, shining through the Forever, through the Eternal, through the Always.

Trading Specialness for True Sight

May 2

You want to be the most special. In some corner of your world or in all corners of your world you want to be the best. Or the worst is good enough too, as long as it stands out in some way from the whole.

It's not You that wants this. Thank goodness it is just the fabricated part of you, the ego, that wants specialness. YOU, most beautiful thing in the universe want only love and goodness and brightness and union and everything that breaks your heart open over and over again as your weary feet tread on this ancient and long journey back to its heavenly source.

Noticing, seeing the places where you want to be special is mandatory.

Everything about the ego must be exposed. And the base of every human mind has the exact same content. Do you want to be the most loved, the most loving, the best healer, teacher? When you find it, it's not to be dismayed even though it can feel a little shocking at times, how harsh and separating it is. It's just the nature of having an individual self. How can it maintain its individuality? Only through this hierarchy of ways.

Acknowledging this specialness, taking it wholeheartedly to your divine altar where all is transformed. Handing it back, knowing you can't correct it, but the Heart can and will correct everything given to it.

And so we even out the palette of our lives. Our equality and union with all become the most important thing. Through the eyes of the Self, all becomes cleaner, brighter, softer. Our eyes light up when we see our brother or sister. They are no longer the competitor, the enemy, but joining with them becomes the very source of our new-found equanimity of heart.

And we walk a different world now, still a world of dreams but a forgiven world where the soft eyes of the Holy Spirit rest on all we look on. Peace and innocence at last. And the recognition of the exact same peace and innocence in every heart. What would we not endure for this?

Thank You, Transparency

May 20

Keeping certain thoughts private to ourselves keeps us separate from a full communion with everybody and consequently with our Holy Self. It upholds divisiveness and there cannot be true happiness and peace as long as separation wins out.

The ego lives and survives in non-exposure. Through the life there are big things we feel ashamed of and little things we're ashamed of. It really makes no difference, big or small. It's the energy that blocks.

"And yet, it is only the hidden that can terrify, not for what it is but for its hiddenness." ~ *A Course in Miracles*

The content of what we're keeping secret is irrelevant. It is the energetic wall that secrecy creates that keeps us apart.

What a journey it is for all of us to open ourselves up, to let others in completely. But so absolutely necessary and rewarding.

My way to transparency began back in the nineties, when I was a full-time caretaker for my husband with brain cancer. It was an arduous time, my life given over completely to his needs. I knew so little about self-care back then. Before his sickness our marriage was shaky and separation and divorce were lining themselves up. I had great fear of managing on my own, emotionally and financially.

One year into his illness, to my great dismay I realized I was having a lot of thoughts about wanting him to die. That would solve all my problems. No more heavy caretaking and I would be better off financially than if he were alive. I lived with these thoughts for months, feeling like a terrible person. Shame and guilt—my regular companions.

At one point I couldn't take the separation from my husband any longer. I went to him, actually kneeling down in front of him, this tortured soul needing to bare itself. It was one of the most tender, moving moments in my life. How he received me, in full forgiveness. With the brain cancer he didn't have much strength in his hand but with what he had, he stroked my head gently. His speech was greatly affected also but I could make him out to be saying that he would feel the same way if he were in my shoes. It was complete absolution and the release was enormous. The thoughts did revisit for some time but never to the same degree, and I was able to share with friends and recognize the commonality of this human response to intensity and it all became lighter.

We may not all have heavy examples like this. Our learning curve has so much more maturity now but still the tendency can be to want to keep parts of the mind hidden from others. We do ourselves a great kindness as we learn to embrace transparency and let people in. There is nothing richer than these moments of joining with another, baring our hearts, letting the soft tendrils of union wrap themselves around us. Back in that pre-separated state where the gap has closed. Mercy that it is possible. So much mercy.

There Are No Strangers

May 31

Feeling a bit incapacitated this morning and knowing I had to interact over some business with someone I didn't know—the thought came in "I'm not able for strangers now."

On the heels of this, instigated by the heart with a rush of softness and knowing, I could hear and feel "There are no strangers."

Only me. Dear me. Coming to help me in all ways.
The energetic walls of separation keep tumbling down, evaporating, as we let the world in. A world we made of strangers and enemies and shadow puppets we must keep our distance from. But now through our longing for a better way, everyone becomes our friend. Everyone starts to feel at moments as if they are long lost lovers. How grateful we are to receive them. How dry and lonely we have been without them.

We sit here, snug in our heart. Greeting a world of friends. A world of you. Receiving thankfully all the goodness they bring. A bounty of heart.

And if this is not our reality in this moment and we are in a phase of ego purging, numbness, dryness, it can help a lot to renew our commitment to whatever it is the heart truly longs for. Your prayer of the heart. What is the desire that sits at the center of your being? Offering this to your Holy Self has a way of reorienting your mind to the only thing that's important. It's as if you're on this crooked line to nowhere and remembering what you really want catapults you out of lostness and confusion and onto a straight line to heaven.

Its completion is inevitable. How blessed we are to be on our Way. A good Way. A holy Way. A right-minded Way. On this

Way we know no strangers. Only a brother or sister equally alight in truth. Equally shining their Holy Being. For the eyes and heart that can see.

Let the Holy Spirit Do the Heavy Lifting

June 12

Such a strong tendency to believe we have to do all the heavy work of unraveling. That we have to figure out what is going on when we are disturbed and triggered. That we have to strain and struggle with the mud in the mind, trying to clear it out of our consciousness. That "we" have to do this. It's not going to clear unless "we" keep trying to understand it and resolve it.

This is the ego trying to cleanse the ego.

But there is something else at hand, way more powerful, knowledgeable and far seeing and that is the Holy Spirit, our true Self. Its function is to receive the turbulence and the confusion. Willingly given up by the mind in the recognition that this is its resolution. The Holy Spirit takes back. How simple it is really. We empty ourselves of the nonsense; the Holy Spirit airlifts it away. Even if you don't feel this immediately, trust in what is happening and the eventual lightness that comes. You can be buoyed up by this knowing. Another blessed layer of unconscious material is disappearing into the heart of God.

"Never approach the holy instant after you have tried to remove all fear and hatred from your mind. That is its function. Never attempt to overlook your guilt before you ask the Holy Spirit's help. That is His function. Your part is only to offer Him a little willingness to let Him remove all fear and hatred, and to be forgiven." ~ *A Course in Miracles*

Anything, anything at all you don't want in your consciousness: how wonderful to remember that's all that's needed, to not want this foreign, separating material residing in your most divine Self. You give it back with a simple "I don't want this anymore." It is the absolute joy of the Self to relieve you of it.

Why wait any longer? Let today be the day we let the Holy Spirit do the heavy lifting.

Maybe the Last Thing to Go

July 7

For years now, I have been sitting with sickness. I've been all over the map, body declining, on hospice, getting better, off hospice. All to be repeated again later.

I have felt the attraction to death as a way out of this situation. I have felt the fear of death many, many times over. Not wanting to leave the familiarity of my body, the familiarity of things and loved ones around me. The odd feeling of safety that being in a body seems to give.

I have longed for the body to get better so I could be out of this situation even as, at the same time, I had great doubts as to how a miracle could happen to transform the apparent, poorly shape the body was in.

It takes time and much, much processing, it seems, to let go of the investment in the welfare of the body. To learn to fly free, to be able to hold a state in your mind where you know it's all okay either way. You live, you die, you get better, you don't get better. To arrive at the place where the overriding knowing is that you are Spirit. You're not this body. And its welfare is not your concern.

No need to touch thoughts about diet and medicine and therapies or what could help or what you are doing wrong or what beliefs you're still clinging to that are sabotaging your physical healing. You are beyond that now. And this feeling that's alive in your chest, that's not going anywhere—this is Home.

And Home is precious Home. And oh, how very precious is this Home. The real settling at last. Home is not going anywhere and you are not going anywhere from Home. Home is in charge. Even as it seems to breathe you, in and out, with the same simplicity that it views all the movements, people, situations. All just appearing and disappearing. It can be that light and undisturbing. Home doesn't mind about anything. Whether there's a body there or not.

Maybe it is the last thing to go… this investment in the body's welfare.

And until this becomes our lived experience, can we welcome all the circumstances of present daily living that are gradually and kindly taking us there? Letting all things be exactly as they are. Learning to relinquish our interest in the dream. And it takes the time it takes. Letting go of any self-judgment around time and failure. Perhaps you are triggered and worked up and having to sit with intensity of sensation and emotion. So be it. It is the burning away of illusion. You return clearer, brighter, emptier of dense mind.

Focusing on Home and Light and Holiness in you and all who arise in your mind, spend time with you or breeze by you. The path of the sages before you. The path of the free. The glorious path of you.

"Here is my secret: I don't mind what happens."

~ Jiddu Krishnamurti

The Self Is So Clean!

July 25

Reflecting on this whole phenomenon of people pleasing and how rampant it still is in so many of us, I was alerted to the truth with the statement, the Self is so clean! For a few moments I could feel how clear and direct the Self is.

It doesn't go around rooting into the dream, looking for non-existent people to say something nice to, so that you feel good about yourself. So that your own character gets to feel good. For a flash, she feels a little more loved, special, gets to bask in a certain glow that is familiar and pleasant but fades away again quite quickly.

Years of childhood conditioning to be good and kind and obedient and helpful: How do we let go of this? How do we even begin to decipher what words and behaviors are coming from the conditioned self and what are coming from the newly opening heart where it feels like the most natural thing in the world to be kind, to say kind things, to smile, laugh, invite, ignite that state of well-being in others?

After much time of watching this people-pleasing concept in myself, I can say there is no easy answer to this. It is truly a gradual process of discernment for each of us. It is a slight stopping, seeing what's on the tip of the tongue that's wanting to be said. A stopping. A waiting. Is this the Self? Is this clean?

Not clean as opposed to "dirty." There is nothing dirty. Just the quality, the brightness, the clarity of "clean."

Stopping and waiting will be uncomfortable. This is where the conditioned persona normally rushes in with some remark that establishes pleasantness, agreement, connection. Stopping is big. The survival tactics of the ego are interrupted. So we must learn to hold tight for a while and when we can't do that, let us be gentle and understanding with ourselves. It is so much bigger than it looks. You are breaking the cycle of seeking love externally, in the dream—a barren land.

It's the garden of your own heart that you want to replenish. Not that it needs replenishing because it cannot empty; it needs claiming as the Oasis it is.

Pray for guidance here. Get the Holy Spirit on your side. Show your clear intention to no longer be fooled by the games of the mythical "me." You want the strength of Spirit that stands tall and clean, not the bending, looping, "I'll say whatever you want to hear so you'll love me." You're on your way. The outcome is always inevitable when the Holy Spirit's help has been invited in.

You are the Light of God. Not the dullness of made-up images in your dream of subservience and seeking.

You Are the Streaming Christ

July 30

This may seem like a tall order, but we have made such small orders of ourselves for so long that it now seems incredibly arrogant to proclaim the Truth of our being.

You are the streaming light of Christ. Infinite light.

Perhaps this is just known semi-conceptually from the taking in of spiritual teachings, or you've had glimpses of it, or you've landed on the revelationary truth of it that you cannot forget or begin to argue with. Revelations that have been fully seen and felt and that's your Base that you can return to at moments when needed.

For myself, on an ayahuasca journey I did many moons ago, I was graced to see the nature of Reality. When I was brought deep into myself, I discovered there was no Jesus, no Ramana, no Pema, no teacher or student or individual. Just this all-pervasive peace and light and stillness. This Truth was riveting at the time and any argument the mind might come up with that this was unreal would be just laughable.

We "know" to some degree that's who we are but most of us are still living out of conditioned mind. Living out of beliefs, primarily that of a separated, individual self, and believing that the body is real.

How can we bring more aliveness into knowing who we are? Make it an everyday, lived experience. How can we step out of the humdrum struggle of the character, this mythical me?

We can STEP OUT.

And we STEP OUT completely. We go from the gluey stickiness of the persona to the radiant Light of what you are. No half-measures. Half-measures will pull you back down in no time.

My favorite way of establishing myself as Light is to start blessing everything, particularly whoever is in front of me, whoever comes to my mind.

Choose your own blessing words, the ones that light you up a bit, that have a transmission from your heart, from the Holy Spirit, just for you, often unique to you.

I start out with saying silently *I bless you.* This orients me into a different state of mind. Out of the human, into the divine.

I bow to you. I find this to be potent. The thought of bowing reminds me of who and what exactly I am in front of. Not a body, not a character with flaws that I may have been judging.

It takes the *Namaste* greeting very seriously and lifts my mind into the awareness of the divinity of this being in front of me. If I'm seeing divinity there, I'm feeling divinity here in my own self. I have stepped out.

I "Light" you. I "Christ" you.

In the same vein, to "Christ" someone is to let the presenting body, image, appearance fade away and to imagine the shining Light they are in Truth. No need to muddle your mind about how well you're seeing this Light. This will wake up more in time, in your own evolution. Here, you are directing traffic, training the mind in where you want it to go, to see the face of Christ in all.

There is no need to discriminate between our brothers. How evolved they are. It's all the same, whether they have a so-called holy life or dark life. The light of Christ shines as brilliantly in every being no matter what role they've taken on. It's just someone playing out his or her karma who has no idea of who they are in Truth. But YOU know. Thank God you know. And it is our job, our function to lift, to raise the whole.

Find the Light in your brother. Find that Light. It's all you're here for, my sweet one. All you are here for. To find his Light, to see his Light is to see your own. And you are Home.

You are the streaming Christ. Let that Light that you are gradually explode, take over all sense of form and matter, over and over again, until at a moment's notice, in one holy instant you can STEP OUT of illusion, no matter what is going on in your dream.

No such thing as a tall order. Just the Truth of our being.

APPENDICES

Steps to Forgiveness

from The Vibrant Heart Blog

The deeper premise of this forgiveness work is based on the non-dual understanding that this world of form and matter and separation is an illusion of mind. That there is only Oneness—in spirit, not in form. That we have never left our Source and we but dream this mental dream of judgment, projection, blame and conflict.

I have used these steps these past years and have found them to be very freeing. The way they are outlined may not necessarily work for you, so feel free to play with them and adjust to your own heart's way. Strong karmic pieces do not move easily, and you may need to repeat these steps many, many times over. Don't think they are not working or that nothing is happening. Each time you do this you are releasing another layer of illusion and slowly, gradually full release from the world you made is experienced. And the happiness, love and light that you are makes itself known and lived in you.

You are learning to forgive your brother for "what he did not do." Because it is all imagined. It has no reality.

When you notice you're triggered by a person or circumstance:

1. You remember this is your dream. You made this up.

(Just saying this slowly to yourself several times over—*I made this up—I made this up*—trying to take it in—you are already half-way out of the vise of victim.)

2. What is this making you feel? Irritated, angry, betrayed, bereft, left out of the love or goodness, less than, etc. Determine what you feel and believe.

(These feelings and states of mind are already inside me and are being projected out, making this scenario happen. These beliefs are creating MY dream. I project what's in here, and then I perceive the same. It has NOTHING to do with the person or the event. This part is so important, shifting the source of the disturbance from the external to the internal. Of course, it is challenging at first, but stick with it. The rewards are so great.)

3. You remember where these feelings are coming from.

(Now that you've brought back the projection entirely inside you, you look at the source of the angst. It is all coming from the original, collective guilt and pain of separation from God. It will undoubtedly be replaying events and feelings from childhood, from past lives, and these may well surface and come to mind, but underneath all of that, it is the pain of the loss of Love, the pain of finding ourselves kicked out of Heaven.

I can't tell you how wonderful and clear it is to make this connection. It may start out as an intellectual awareness, but after a while it will become an experience and more easily accessible.)

4. Sit for a while with any contraction that's appearing in the body, any release of emotion that wants to happen. Just keep making the connection between the present pain and the original loss of Father/Mother.

5. Now you give it all back to God, to your Holy Self, to the Holy Spirit. To Ramana, to Jesus, to your heart's favorite sage.

(You hand it over. You don't want separation anymore. You bring the darkness to the light. You lay it all at the altar of your heart. If you like, you can imagine giving it over into sacred hands of light. This step is the easiest because your work is done, your Holy Self takes over, and it is actually Spirit that takes care of the undoing. All that was needed was your willingness and intention.)

6. Thank the Holy Spirit for healing your mind.

(This is beautiful to do because again, it is an acknowledgment that He is taking care of it, not you as a self-concept. And it is an acknowledgment that it is being undone; it is already undone. Your brother is innocent, and you are innocent because nothing ever happened.)

From Darkness to Light

In March, 2020, Grace Bubeck interviewed me for her series Seekers Finders: interviews with "ordinary" people about their spiritual journey. https://youtu.be/TR-hZ6al6dE

It was lovely for me to do this with Grace. Some of the topics covered:

- how my journey began

- how *A Course in Miracles* came to me and its effect

- the impact of having Devaji as a teacher

- sickness, hospice as a classroom

- what have I learned/found

Love to all, Pema

Acknowledgments

To my beloved teacher, Jesus, whatever you are exactly. It is your hand I hold, your heart I rest in and your teachings in *A Course in Miracles* that pull me ever more deeply into the Heart and Light of God.

My beautiful daughters, Orna and Amaya, for your incredible love and support. What a lucky mother to have friendship, companionship, and intimacy mark the nature of our relationship. Dedicating yourselves to taking care of this form through several bouts of serious illness. Giving yourselves over to the tender beauty and grind of everyday caretaking. How can I possibly thank you? You both mean the world to me.

My dearest siblings who have supported me in many ways, especially financially in this life. Thank you from the bottom of my heart for the safety, comfort, and ease you brought me.

My beloved friend and mentor, Faith Boyarin, who took me under her loving, maternal wing when I first moved to Portland, Oregon. It felt like my first experience of truly being loved and cared for. You sustained me through the dark times, dearest Faith. Always there for me. I couldn't have done it without you.

Devaji, who lit the path for me, loved me into a very necessary healing and so many times jollied me out of dark states of mind with the vibrancy of Truth. You taught me how to be "at play in the fields of the Lord."

Anandi Ramana, my dearest friend, who showed up for me in an ayahuasca journey as an Angel. "Anandi is an Angel" is what I heard. This book could not have seen the light of day without you. Thank you for masterminding its creation and for all the encouragement and love that flows effortlessly from your awakened heart.

And a big thank you to dearest Praseela for bringing a fresh, capable, and corrective eye to the final editing. As she does with so much in our community. A blessed being.

My guide and mentor, Coreen Walson. Your wonderful spark of light that ignited my own. Your clear mind reaching into mine, with the help of Jesus, and miracles happen. I love you, Coreen.

And words can't touch the beauty of my sangha family in Mt. Shasta and all over. What a blessed life to have such a community of resonant, awakening beings. Such gifts of deep friendship and connection. Thank you for all your incredible love and support.

Praise for Pema

"Beautifully spoken, luminous truth. Thank you, Pema dear, for continuously shining this Light. My love and gratitude to you, a thousand times over for sharing such kindness and compassionate truth."

~ Ashana Kawainui, International Music Artist

"Pema's writing blows me away. Every expression from her is pure light."

~ Lisa Natoli, *A Course in Miracles* teacher,
Teachers of God Foundation

"Pema has such a gift for embodying Spirit through the letter. Her inspired writings have the blessed ability to bypass the egoic thinking and its defenses and land square within our hearts."

~ Coreen Walson, *A Course in Miracles* teacher,
"Take Me to Truth"

"Pema's words are spicy salve, waking up and soothing all at once."

~ KS

"Pema is a true mystical miracle. Born into a difficult environment she has transformed the darkness into pure radiant light. Every being that knows her loves her. Her heart's ability to hold the space of kindness and love is unprecedented.

Over her life she transformed from someone in deep fear into the fearless presence of pure compassion for all humanity. All who have had the grace to know her have been inspired by and guided from this loving place of pure humility. She has withstood the rigors of terminal cancer with nothing but receptivity, gratitude and elegance.

The two traits that stand out most in Pema's presence are total unconditional Love and complete humility. One of her endless gifts is through her honest writings of her own direct experience which can be a guiding post for all seekers. Every single person in our spiritual community reveres the boundless gifts that move through her. From the onset of the cancer diagnosis and through all the enormous challenges it brought forth, she has maintained this as only a gift from God, not only welcoming the cancer but appreciating its gifts. She is a living embodiment of what is possible in a human life in its highest order.

This book has great pearls to offer and can only soften the Heart and open the doorway to Divine Love."

~ Devaji, A Non-Dual Spiritual Teacher

Made in the USA
Las Vegas, NV
20 August 2021